TABLE OF CONTENTS

THE MYSTERY OF
TRANSFORMING LOVE

By

ADRIAN VAN KAAM, C.S.Sp.

DIMENSION BOOKS
Denville, New Jersey 07834

Imprimi Protest: *Rev. Philip J. Haggerty, C.S.Sp.*
Provincial

Nihil Obstat: *Rev. William J. Winter, S.T.D.*
Censor Librorum

Imprimatur: *Most Rev. Vincent M. Leonard, D.D.*
Bishop of Pittsburgh

December 1, 1981

Published by

DIMENSION BOOKS INC.
PO Box 811
Denville NJ 07834-0811

ISBN 0-87193-176-1 Hardcover
ISBN 0-87193-182-6 Paperback

PREFACE

This book is a sequence to *LOOKING FOR JESUS,* a series of meditations on the first part of the Farewell Discourse in the Gospel of St. John. The meditations in this volume deal with the final part of this Discourse.

The new title is *THE MYSTERY OF TRANS-FORMING LOVE.* It may be helpful for the reader to know how this mystery of transformation fits into the science of formative spirituality developed by the author and his colleagues at the graduate Institute of Formative Spirituality at Duquesne University.

To understand the science of human and Christian formation, we must reflect on the deepest question about formation that each of us may raise, at least implicitly. Our response to it colors all our responses to the particular formation questions that are evoked by our daily experiences. In other words our basic answer will profoundly affect our personal formation history. Our whole existence and that of the globe on which we have to give form to life and world is somehow subject to the meaning of the mystery of formation.

We could speak about a threefold epiphany of the formation mystery. This mystery discloses itself in three main ways: the cosmic, the human, and the transhuman. Let us consider first of all the cosmic epiphany of the formation mystery. What is the secret of the foundational consonance of the cosmos? Recent discoveries reveal to us where that secret resides. They point to the atomic and subatomic, cosmic dance of ever ongoing formation and reformation in the universe. This has led to the view that the cosmos is an all embracing energy process of continuous interformation. This is true not only of the macro but also of the microcosmos, which guides even the most minute form changes in the organismic cells of our brain, nervous system and other organs. Our life formation thus shares in each of its cells in this dance of interformation of formation energies.

The same mystery of formation is the source not only of its cosmic but also of its distinctively human epiphany. This manifestation takes place in the uniquely transcendent dimension of our foundational human life form. It is this human epiphany which explains why we surpass the mere cosmic manifestation of the formation mystery. Yet this does not mean that we can deny the continuous cosmic epiphany of the formation mystery in our life and world. We cannot authentically speak about human formation without constantly referring, at least implicitly, to the cosmic interformation process in which we are inserted from conception to death. Fortunately, there is no contradiction, only complementarity, between the three epiphanies of the formation mystery.

Both the cosmic and the mere human formative epiphanies of the mystery of formation are not sufficient to grant us the peace and joy of a fully consonant formation of our human life. This insufficiency is, of course, not due to a lack of form potency in these created divine gifts themselves. We ourselves are the cause of their lack of effectiveness. The original Fall led to the emergence in our life of the pride-form, which tempts us with the illusion that by ourselves alone we can give and receive form in our life and world. In other words, the autarchic pride form may create the exalted illusion that we alone are the source of the formation of life and world. At times we may transcend such exaltation of the pride form. Then we become able to acknowledge that forming divine energies continuously influence the cosmic and cultural fields of formation from which we emerge continuously. This enlightenment enables us to appraise such manifestations of the divine form energies wisely and to enlist them firmly and gently in service of our congenial and compatible life formation. We are free then from the spell of exaltations. We break the bonds of the autarchic pride form. We begin to experience, concretely and personally, that every formation including our own somehow participates in the cosmic and human epiphanies of the mystery of formation.

The experience of liberation from the pride-form not only opens us up to the mystery of formation; it saves us from our sterile isolation; it inspires us to flow with the divine formation energies in quiet consonance. In the measure that such consonance becomes ours we experience more equanimity inwardly. There are innumerable ways that facilitate such liberation. Hence we see a variety of formation exercises developed in the many formation traditions of humanity.

The mystery of formation teaches us that all forms in and around us are impermanent and transitory. Our pride-form, on the contrary, gives rise to elated images of permanence, or else it makes us refuse the constant acknowledgement of the fleetingness of our life and its passing achievements. Our life forms too are current. We have to grow from current life form to current life form to become what we are foundationally called to be. When it is given to us to realize our own foundational life form, it will not be lasting within this physical universe; death comes like a thief in the night to take that form away. All forms in the universe emerge and pass away, also each human form.

To face the fact that flow and change are foundational features of all formation is painful as long as we live in the shadow of the pride-form. We are secretly inclined to be proud and possessive of the current forms we receive or give to our life and surroundings. In fear of losing them we resist the epiphanous flow of the mystery of formation. We try to cling to fixed forms of life and world. We do not acknowledge that to attach ourselves to them as ultimate is to become enslaved to idolize exaltations that sooner or later will fade away like all forms in this cosmos. Such idolizing of vanishing forms makes us vulnerable to anything that will threaten their continuation. It sets us up for the kind of unnecessary, deformative suffering that results from the enchantment by changeable forms of life and world. Deformative suffering will be our fate when we resist the epiphanous flow of formation, when we try to encapsulate ourselves in the forms of an enchanted world we have exalted beyond its limited power, beauty and meaning.

The root of such idolizing is any frantic clinging to the exalted primordial fantasy of the pride-form.

This fantasy suggests that our functional ego is a separate power of formation fiercely independent of any other formation power in which the mystery of formation appears and calls us forth silently. To cling to that exalted self-image leads to the same fixation as the idolizing of any other fixed form we have attained in life or world.

Our ignorance of the mystery of formation and its epiphanies tempts us to imagine that we can receive form or give form to life and world in merely functional inner and outer ways of control and manipulation. The more people are able to transcend this illusion of total self-sufficiency, the more they will be able to coform their lives in consonance with the flow of the formation mystery. Such coformation presupposes the ability to wait upon its disclosures, to go alone with its concealment or its disclosure in equanimity, to persevere in times of distress and to be modest and cautious in times of achievement. This attitude fosters gentleness of mind and heart which avoids excess, extravagance, and indulgence. It prefers to leave things undone to overdoing them. Its main concern is to remain in consonance with the epiphanies of the mystery of formation.

Such consonance contributes to the disclosure of appropriate form directives. Impatient overdoing of things may spawn fast and impressive accomplishments while one loses the wise and healing way of consonance. The heady wine of acclaim and applause cannot make up for the loss of consonant form direction and the tragedy of missing out on one's foundational life vocation.

Abandonment to the mystery of formation becomes for the Christian an abandonment to the transhuman epiphany of that mystery. The history of formation has taught humanity abundantly that it cannot attain the consonance we have described by a free and continuous collaboration with the cosmic and human epiphanies of this mystery. Since the Fall the pride-form has too strong a hold on human formation to prevent repeated failure in receptivity to the created divine formation powers. It is only through the mystery of transforming love revealed and communicated in Christ that we can hope to attain this consonance with the divine created formation powers.

The Christ-form of the soul enables us to die to the pride-form that is the source of our tragic condition. This mystery of transforming love inspires us daily to share in its transforming presence, also in its micro and macrocosmic manifestations. It asks us to flow with it no matter what we do. We are called to experience this epiphany of the mystery of transforming love in the small events that bind our days together. It wants to awaken us to its presence in the midst of everydayness. Everyday life itself in its simple Nazareth atmosphere is our privileged opening to the mystery of transformation.

Such deepened awareness is the secret of a life formation that can be at the same time highly functional and profoundly mystical. Transforming love enables us to function well in the present with full and loving attention to the seemingly small and pedestrian course daily life entails. Simultaneously this transforming love enables us to experience the marvel of passing things and little tasks in the light of the mystery that formatively maintains their flow and illumines their pneumatic meaning in our hearts and minds.

Preface

At some graced moments we may feel like softly singing inwardly: How wondrous, how mysterious! I eat food, I write words, I walk, I converse, I water flowers, I clean my room, I make the bed, I wash my hands, I feel the sun, the rain, the wind, the snow. In all these things I sense and live the transforming love of Jesus of Nazareth, who experiences in and with me the delight of loving obedience to the Father's will manifested in this everydayness. Such experiences remind us of similar ones recorded in the psalms of the Hebrew formation tradition and in the words of the Farewell Discourse.

The mystery of transforming love allows one's everyday life to be formed congenially, compatibly and compassionately by the marvel of providential interaction that emerges from one's life and formation situation. It helps us to flow simply with the messages of our own life that God allows. When joyful, we smile. When grieving, we cry. When rested, we labor again. When tired, we rest. But we do it all in consonance with the mystery of transforming love that helps us to respond in gentle obedience to these experiences.

The mystery of transforming love makes us transcend our functionalistic willfulness. This willfulness destroys our natural consonance with the cosmic and human epiphany of the formation mystery. It made humanity fall away from its original innocence and consonant attunement to the universal mystery of formation. The mystery of transforming love helps us to regain that *attunement* by *atonement* which is the renewal of *at-one-ment* with the formation mystery we lost sight of in our life. Abandonment to the transhuman epiphany of the formation mystery enables us to disclose the foundational life form to which we are called uniquely.

It is the intention of this book to facilitate the restoration of this consonance by meditation on the revelations of God's transforming love in Christ as contained in Jesus' parting words to his disciples. The author hopes that these meditations may help each reader to come in closer contact with the mystery of transforming love permeating cosmic and human formation and elevating them beyond any formation power humanity could have imagined.

CHAPTER ONE

PRESENCE AND PRUNING
IN THE SPIRITUAL LIFE

"I am the true vine,
and my Father is the vinedresser.
Every branch in me that bears no fruit
he cuts away,
and every branch that does bear fruit he prunes
to make it bear even more.
You are pruned already,
by means of the word that I have spoken to you.
Make your home in me, as I make mine in you.

(Jn. 15:1-4)

The meal is ended. Jesus tells them gently:
"Come now, let us go." *(Jn.* 14:31) Reluctantly they
rise from their couches. They hesitate to break the
spell of his words. They linger on in the expectation
of more. Jesus looks at them with compassion. They
will have to cope with a mean and hostile world. He
begins to urge them to remain with him in the midst
of persecution. Faith in him will keep their life vibrant
in spite of his departure. No matter the intimidation,
they should foster the graced unfolding of humanity;
they should bear his fruit in the garden of the history

of human formation. He assures them that his leaving does not mean the end.

When the leader of a small band of people is executed it may be the end of his movement. The group disperses in fear of what may be done to them. Disappointed they flee back to their jobs and families. It is all over. Jesus wants to prevent this loss of hope. He had already consoled them in many ways: where he is going they will also go when the time is ripe; another helper will be sent to them, the Holy Spirit; even he himself will return.

These last poignant moments, however, he promises something different and unexpected. He no longer speaks of leaving but of remaining. He asks them to remain in him: "Make your home in me, as I make mine in you."

How delighted we are when a good friend keeps us company. We know it cannot last. When his departure is near we beg him to stay. He may stay for an hour, perhaps a few hours, a few days, a week but it cannot last forever. There will always be an end. We feel this most deeply when death cuts a loved one out of our lives. We can no longer beseech him to stay; death is the end of staying. That is true, too, of the bodily presence of Jesus.

To be with Jesus still means for the disciples that they see him among them, that he eats and drinks with them, walks with them the roads of Israel and talks to the people they meet on the way. He begins to speak now about another kind of presence, strange and unheard of. How can you make your home in another person while that other person makes his home in you? To help them understand Jesus gropes for a comparison. Fond of nature, the picture of a sturdy vine and its branches dense with luscious grapes springs to his lively imagination. Maybe his loving eyes caught at this moment in wonder a vine with tendrils spreading near an open window of the room. Maybe he remembered the vineyards he passed during his travels while vinedressers were pruning the branches, gathering those that had died. Or the image of the vine may have been inspired by the Passover blessings spoken at the meal. In one of them wine is hailed as "the fruit of the vine." As a devout son of Israel Jesus was familiar with the image of the vine in the Scriptures he had meditated upon since his youth. He had encountered it in the writings of Isaiah (5:1), the Psalmist (80:8), and Jeremiah (2:21). Now He adopts their image in an original way, filling it with new meaning.

He images himself as a vine and the disciples as his branches. But it is more than imagery. He says: I *am* the true vine. Jesus is not merely like a vine. He is our vine, our real source of divine life. The vine in the vineyard is only a shadow of what Jesus' life-giving power means in our lives.

False prophets may claim that they are the vine or the source of forming truth and life for people. Jesus calls himself the *true* vine. He alone is the real source of forming truth and life for all of us.

We are the branches. Inserted in Jesus, the vine, we are brimming with the sap of life; we can carry blossom and fruit. Outside the vine we wither away. We are no strangers to Jesus. He knows us intimately; daily we touch him, for we are already planted within him through baptism. He shares with us his own life and its miraculous power to bring forth abundant fruit in history. To his apostles, however, he does not speak about baptism. Instead he says to them: "You are pruned already by means of the word that I have spoken to you."

The apostles had not been baptized. The baptism of Jesus could only be given after his death and resurrection. Baptism replaces for us what the disciples received by their graced interaction with Jesus filling them daily with the power and beauty of his forming word. That is what Jesus meant when he said that the word had pruned them already.

His word has to prune us, too. Nobody can stay a disciple of Jesus without allowing Jesus' word to prune him. I can bear his fruit in the measure that I allow his word to be a power of formation in my life. Not everything I do or say is a fruit of Jesus' presence. The Father wants my life to take its own divine direction. Only those deeds of mine that obey the Father's orientation for me are the fruits of the vine. Such fruits transform me into the unique image of the Lord he meant me to be. I must allow the Father to prune the branch I am into a form that can yield the special fruits he wants me to bear for suffering humanity.

Jesus says, therefore: "My Father is the vine-dresser." If we are to bear the sweet grapes of love, kindness, and humility we need to be pruned. We have to be so rooted in the vine, Jesus, that when the Father sees us, the branches, he sees Jesus himself. When he bends over Jesus in love, he bends over us. The Father does not have to be concerned if the vine itself is growing properly. We, the outgrowths of the vine, are his concern. He has to prune us constantly.

During Jesus' life on earth the vinedresser did "dress" him — he prepared Jesus for sacrifice. The Father makes us ready for suffering too. Even if we bear fruit, he trims us that we may bear more. Dryness in prayer may be a sign that the Father is trimming us inwardly. Difficulties in life may be seen as opportunities to be pruned by the Father.

This fatherly pruning or formation takes place mostly in the small events that make up my day. Health and sickness, understanding and misunderstanding, rejection and acceptance — the divine pruner uses them all to transform steadily my resistant soul. To know the meaning of Father's pruning and my response to it, I must resort to the pruning power of the word. Jesus' word prunes my misunderstanding of Father's deeds in my life. I must dwell on the words of Jesus. They are my light on the way. Therefore Jesus says: "If you remain in me and my words remain in you." *(Jn.* 15:7)

Thank you for staying with me, Lord Jesus. If I had to remain in you by my force alone, I would soon betray your presence. You tenderly implanted me into yourself by the miracle of baptism. How often I broke my oneness with you and hindered its unfolding. But you constantly restored the loving union that was lost. You attracted me; you permeated me with the sweet scent of your presence. I beg you, Lord Jesus, let your silent presence in me be a power of transformation.

I hear you whisper in my soul: remain in me, then I will remain in you. Your loyalty to me, my Lord, can never be questioned. You are fidelity itself. You loved me and pruned me before I could love you. Your acceptance of me is not hemmed in by impossible conditions. You are all for me even when I am against you. You cherish me no matter how I feel or am. It is only I who can be unfaithful to you. Therefore you have to ask me: "Remain in me." You assure me once and for all: "Then I will remain in you."

How direct and simple is the promise of your presence. You don't tell me that it is anything out of the ordinary. It is not a question of elated experiences. They may or may not accompany your presence in me. Your presence is not only for people more exalted than I, people unusually graced and gifted. It is also for me, a simple believer in your daily love and care.

To remain in you is not a feat of feeling or perfection. To remain in you is to believe in you, to surrender to you in faith, hope, and love. When I ask to remain in you, I ask for a special dimension of the grace of faith, the dimension of faith that is fidelity. Please, Lord, let faith and fidelity abound in me; let them fill the empty spaces of my life.

THE STEM OF BETHLEHEM

You are the stem
Of Bethlehem.
Wounded humanity
You made your home.
No longer alone
To cope
With the meanness
Of this life
You make us hope:
We shall arrive
At the shore
Of the land of peace
In the core
Of our being.
We have been fleeing
Your invitation
To be your branch.
The temptation
To self sufficiency
Suffocates its luster.
Make us muster
The wisdom to make
Our home in you.
The luscious grapes
Of your vine
Lovingly drape
The garden of history.
Its tendrils spread
Fertile and tenderly
In the hearts of people
Outside this stem
Of Bethlehem
We crumble,
We wither away
Day after day
In idle illusion.

CHAPTER TWO

FRUITS OF VULNERABLE BRANCHES

I am the true vine,
and my Father is the vinedresser.

(Jn. 15:1)

Make your home in me, as I make mine in you.
As a branch cannot bear fruit all by itself,
but must remain part of the vine,
neither can you unless you remain in me.
I am the vine,
you are the branches.
Whoever remains in me, with me in him,
bears fruit in plenty;
for cut off from me you can do nothing.
Anyone who does not remain in me
is like a branch that has been thrown away
he withers;
these branches are collected and thrown on the fire,
and they are burned.
If you remain in me
and my words remain in you,
you may ask what you will
and you shall get it.

(Jn. 15:4-7)

As a dedicated son of Israel Jesus had meditated continuously the Hebrew scriptures. Israel was described there as the chosen vine of Yaweh. *(Ps.* 80:8-16; *Jr.* 2:21; *Ezk.* 15;19:10; *Ho.* 10:11) The vine had become a beloved symbol of Israel. It was engraved, for instance, on the coins of the Macabees. Yet reading the scriptures as a devout young man, Jesus had found that this vine was condemned as lacking in fidelity to Yahweh. Faithless Israel was compared with a branch that is burned with fire *(Ps.* 80:16), turn up in fury, flung to the ground, withered up, devoured by fire. *(Ezk.* 19:12)

In contrast to this faithless vine, Jesus called himself the "true" vine. He applies here to himself exclusively an image that up to now had been used only of a whole people. No righteous Israelite had ever dared to do the same: to put himself over and above the chosen vine, Israel, as the only true vine in person. It is one of Jesus' plain and forthright revelations of who he is and of what he really means in the history of humanity. "I am the true vine" is one of the striking "I am" statements of the Gospel of St. John.

Jesus may have thought of the song of the psalmist: You transplanted a vine from Egypt; you drove away the nations and planted it. You cleared the ground for it, and it took root and filled the land. The mountains were hidden in its shadow; by its branches the cedars of God. It put forth its foliage to the Sea, its shoots as far as the River. *(Ps.* 80:9-12)

Thank you, Father, for planting the vine of your chosen people in Israel. Thank you infinitely more for bringing the vine, Jesus, out of eternity into time, out of heaven to earth, out of the Trinity into humanity. This transplant is a mystery of love that can never be fathomed by our meagre minds. Thank you, Holy

Vine, for taking root among us, for filling our hearts and humanity and its history, for hiding the mountains of our arrogance in your shadow.

This night before his suffering and death Jesus announces the new beginning of his life in us. He uses the vine-image of the Hebrew scriptures to make clear to these men from Israel his ongoing miraculous presence in their lives, in the lives of all Christians to come. His new presence among us reminds us of a parable in the Syriac Apocalypse of Baruch (2 *Br.* 37-39). This passage tells us about a vine that could speak. It opened his mouth, spoke and destroyed the Cedar. The Cedar in this story personifies the prince of iniquities; the vine, the Messiah.

God has planted you as the true vine among us. You are a vine that speaks to our hearts. Your word invites us to become your branches; it destroys the tall Cedar of our iniquities. The purpose of this mystical union is that we should bear fruit in plenty. To bear this fruit we must live with you daily in sadness and joy, stillness and action, victory and defeat, suffering, death and resurrection. You invite us to spend ourselves so that others might share your message and your life.

As a branch of Jesus, each of us is a new creation. To be his branch by baptism is to be basically a changed person. The vine calls us forth to a life we could never live by the power of nature alone. We are a whole new rung on the ladder of evolution. The grace that comes to us from the vine can change our pulsations, drives, ambitions and aspirations. We are open to inspirations of the Spirit. We are empowered to become men and women of new longings, possibilities and achievements. As members of the body of Christ we are invited to lend him our spirit, mind, heart, eyes, ears, feet and hands, to enable him to be a transforming presence in our surroundings.

To be a branch that bears the transforming presence of Jesus is not so much a question of what we have or do, but of what we are. If a true branch of Jesus nestles itself somewhere in this world things begin to look better. There is less disheartening, less of a chill in the air. Our life affects always the lives of others, inevitably, silently, continuously. Each of us is a center of value radiation. Our impact on others is formative or deformative. It all depends on what our values are. We may be branches of the weed of evil or of the vine Jesus. Our daily comportment is a silent sermon that reverberates in the history of human formation. Hence Jesus declares: "You did not choose me, no, I chose you; and I commissioned you to go out and to bear fruit, fruit that will last." *(Jn.* 15:16)

"I am the vine, you are the branches." It is the vine that draws nourishment from the earth; the vine that spreads the sap of life through the needy branches; the vine that makes it possible for the branches to stay in the vine so that more nourishment may come their way.

Jesus, you make us green and living twigs laden with fruit for all people. Yet we imagine secretly that we can bear fruit by ourselves alone. How we pride ourselves on our clever plans for the betterment of humanity. In our eagerness to implement them we push aside the awareness of your presence. We run here and there. The wheels of our thoughts and feelings are spinning merrily, we act feverishly; yet without you it is all in vain. Our clutching hands will never make your mystery come true in our lives. Detached from you, our little branch hangs loose and limp. If we remain in you, you assure us there will be plenty of fruit. Keep us close to you that our lives may be worthwhile and filled with meaning. Our loyalties are frail; your generosity is infinite. Please hide us in you, Eternal Vine of life and love.

If we don't sink deeply in the eternal vine, we may become trapped in our formation techniques and expect too much from them. We begin to take ourselves too seriously. We feel that we alone are responsible for the coming of the kingdom. If we do not succeed we become upset; we try to force things anxiously. We pretend to be the vine instead of professing we are merely a branch without life of its own. Then, unsure of ourselves, we seek to be assured by the people around us. We become dependent on their praise. If things don't work out well, we feel like a failure. We begin to manipulate others piously. We act as if we ourselves were their vine, their fountain of life, instead of Jesus. We hinder them from growing into unique branches of the Lord. They become copies of us, not images of the Eternal Master.

To be a Christian is to be a minister of Jesus in this world. Ministry can be fruitful only if it is rooted in the mystery of the vine. We have to abide in him. Then, he will transform us more and more in and through our ministry. Remaining in him demands that we often step aside to dwell with him in solitude. Remaining in the vine, Jesus, means believing that we are loved by him no matter what; it is allowing the life and the love of the vine to permeate us and our ministry. It is to minister more by inspiration than by persuasion.

The poet of Psalm 80 tells how the Lord brought a vine from Egypt and planted it. He made it grow and put forth great branches. But the vineyard fence was broken down; the branches were robbed and ravaged by men and beasts. The poet then besieges God to look upon his vine. We pray with Jesus:

Lord of earth and history, look upon the vine you made the new root of humanity. Look upon us, his branches, as we spread and twist all over the world. You know how vulnerable we are to the polluted air of this age of arrogance. To remain in you we need a fence. We need the grace of gentle discipline of image, thought and passion. Otherwise, the fruits of our branches will be robbed and ravaged by worldly distractions. Mend our fences Father so that Jesus' fruits in us will not be stolen or destroyed.

THE SPEAKING VINE

Do not leave me alone
But make your home
In me, my Lord.
Let your word
Be the light
In my night
Of despair
Not knowing where
To find you.
Do not fling to the ground,
Nor turn up in fury
This withered branch
O, give me a chance
For you are the vine
Transplanted in time,
You took root
And filled like a wood
The land and the sky.
Mountains of arrogance
Are hidden in your shadow,
O mighty vine of God.
Your foliage stretches
Over the ages.
Your shoots
Take roots
In willing hearts.
You are a speaking vine,
Your grapes produce the wine
Of wise and mighty words
For tortured souls.
The speaking vine destroys
The cedar of human pride
That rises tall to fight
Your presence on this earth.

CHAPTER THREE

BEARING FRUIT IN DAILY LIFE

Whoever remains in me, with me in him,
bears fruit in plenty;
for cut off from me you can do nothing.

(Jn. 15:5)

It is to the glory of my Father that you should bear
much fruit,
and then you will be my disciples.

(Jn. 15:8)

Jesus speaks about us remaining in him and he remaining in us. What this indwelling should lead to is bearing fruit. Jesus is truly in us. But he is in us not so much as a source of inner experience and spiritual exaltation. He is in us as the principle of our holy fecundity in world and history. He has already told his disciples that we are like a branch in Jesus, but that we cannot remain in him if we don't bear fruit. We must bear fruit in daily life. We must try to function effectively in society. The functional dimension of the human life form is very central in Christianity.

Perhaps no other formation tradition than the Judeo-Christian has put such emphasis on bearing fruit, on functioning well. The incarnational aspect of Christian formation has deepened this dimension of the human life form. To incarnate God concretely in his world implies our functioning in and with Jesus, in ways that make a difference no matter how modestly. This effectiveness is a result of our dwelling in the Lord. At the same time it is the condition of our abiding in him. There is no possibility of our remaining in Jesus without bearing fruit, and we can no longer bear fruit if we are not rooted in him.

The inspirational and the incarnational, the transcendent and the functional aspects of the Christian form of life are interwoven. Remaining and bearing fruit, contemplation and participation, presuppose one another. They form a union of mutual implication.

In this chapter of John both of these words "remaining" and "bearing fruit" are equally important. They appear equally often. As formative readers, we may hesitate between the two. We may ask ourselves: which word contains the most formative message for our unfolding: to bear fruit or to remain? What we can do is to read this chapter, first in a spirit of meditation on Jesus' gentle invitation to remain in him and the promise that goes with it: that we will bear fruit abundantly. Then we may read it again in prayerful reflection on the Lord's loving insistence that we should bear fruit and that remaining in him is the condition of abundant effectiveness in this world.

It is also possible to meditate on this chapter from the perspective of the vine dresser. His ultimate concern is the fruit. It is the aim of all his labor. For him the vine and the branches form a unity. The vine carries its fruits for him. We can ask ourselves what that means for us. With Jesus we form a union that delights our Father in heaven. He does not want to make a distinction between what comes from Jesus and what comes from us. The thing he really cares about is that we bear Jesus' fruit. We complete Jesus' work on earth. We do so in limited and imperfect ways, the vine Jesus in turn completes what is lacking in our fruits due to our imperfections.

Therefore, the vitality of our vine Jesus is emphasized. Not only shall we produce fruit but *much* fruit. At the root of our Christian life formation is the formation of Jesus' life. Jesus lived for the glorification of the Father. The Father is glorified in the works, the fruit of the Son. Glorification means that the truth, the beauty, the splendor and the power of the Eternal Father is shining forth in the work of Jesus. When we abide in Jesus, God will also be glorified by our works, by our fruits. As St. Irenaeus tells us: "The glory of God is man fully alive." This aliveness comes to us from the vine Jesus.

"And then you will be my disciples." The bearing of fruit will manifest ever more that we are true disciples of the Lord. Our Christian life formation is basically a discipleship of Christ; it is to be formed as his disciple more and more. This ongoing formation will be demonstrated in bearing fruit increasingly, in functioning better as graced and gracious servants of a redeemed humanity, in being holy and effective participants in its unfolding history.

What is this remaining in Christ that is the condition of bearing fruit? Does it mean that all of us should have the mystical experiences of the Lord's presence the great masters of Christian formation speak about? We know better. Most of us do not have the gift of ecstacy. Yet, Jesus asks all of us to remain in him. There must be a way of keeping in touch with him that is open to each of us, even the most simple among us. How do we keep in touch with our family, our best friends, our beloved? We do it in many ways: visits, postcards, letters, telephone calls, conversations, a prayer, a memory. It is necessary that we do it often enough to keep the relationship alive.

Remaining in Jesus happens somewhat in the same way. He himself gave the example. The core of his life was keeping in touch with his Father. Time and time again he created a moment of stillness to be alone with God. These moments were flowing over in the rest of his life. He was always abiding with his Father. We can do the same to keep in touch with Jesus. To do so we do not have to be great mystics. It is enough to pay attention to his words as they come to us in our reading of the scriptures, of the words of the liturgy or of the masters of the Christian formation tradition. As soon as a word strikes us, fills us with some peace, we should treasure it in our hearts. We should take it with us in our daily life, come back to it again and again. It is our point of contact with the One who remains in us; it is our way of remaining in Him.

We may make a collection of words and sentences that have proven to be of help in this regard. They can serve as bridges between our busy day and the Lord within us. At any lost moment during the day we may try to remember the words we have chosen as signposts of our presence to him. We should not try to reason about such words in an intellectual way. No, we should allow them gently to penetrate our mind and heart like fragrant oil saturates a dried up sponge. Neither should we be forceful in our attention. It should be a waiting in patience, ready to receive the imprint of the holy word in the depth of our soul, yet also ready to bear with the absence of any consolation. What counts is a steady returning to the words of the Lord by his apostles and saints. This return will keep our will oriented toward him. We are truly abiding in him even if we do not feel or experience the effects of this remaining. Sooner or later he may grant us moments of the experience of his presence. They may be fleeting but precious. When our days are interwoven with such moments of attention we will begin to bear the fruits of kindness and humility, of care and concern, that will make the presence of Jesus known to the world. Then we shall really be experienced as his disciples.

LIKE FRAGRANT OIL

Lord, let me remain in you
Like you remain in me.
Be a source of fruitfulness
In my niche in history.
To carry fruit abundantly
Delights the Father's eye.
He looks at us so tenderly.
And smiles on me,
Alive in you
A servant of humanity.
Fill me with your words,
Those shining bridges
That like rainbows
Harmonize my doings
With the heaven of your presence.
Let them penetrate my busy mind,
My dried up soul,
Like fragrant oil.
If you grant me a fleeting sense
Of your abiding
Let me not clutch it greedily
But flow gently with the mystery
Of your appearance and departure
In my daily life.

CHAPTER FOUR

DIVINE LOVE AS GIFT AND COMMAND

As the Father has loved me,
so I have loved you.

(Jn. 15:9)

We are reflecting on Chapter 15 of the Last Discourse of Jesus. We have seen how our Lord in the beginning of this Chapter directs himself to his disciples with a comparison, poetic and transcendent in its simple beauty. He likens himself to a vine and us to its branches, nourished by his divine vitality.

When we look again at the first part of this Chapter, we realize that after Verse 6 the images of vine and branches are no longer mentioned. Only two other images less intimately connected with this metaphor show up again. Jesus repeats how important it is for our formation to bear fruit in him. He also reminds us anew that we should remain in him. These two teachings of our Lord flow naturally from the imagery of the branches that must remain in the vine to flower out in fruitfulness.

To be sure, these teachings go beyond the image of the vine. We can understand what Jesus means to say to us without knowing about the vine and the branches. We can meditate on the truth of our fruitfulness in union with Jesus without paying attention to that image. Prayerful reflection on remaining in Jesus can by itself give rise to a loving conviction; it can form our heart and foster a life of oneness with him.

One thing is sure: in this passage the most central words for our inner formation are "remaining" and "bearing fruit." These admonishments weave the first half of Chapter 15 (1-17) into a striking unity. The whole of this text consists of two units that are distinctly different, namely, Verses 1-8 and 9-17. These two groups of teachings are bridged by "remaining" and "bearing fruit."

Jesus adds another idea in Verses 9-17. He announces to us a new gift of divine love at the heart of our life. This is neither the first nor the last time that Jesus speaks about divine love in this discourse. We find him speaking like this already in Chapter 14: 15-21 and 23-24. Jesus returns to this gift in Chapter 16: 27 and Chapter 17: 23-24, 26. In this passage, however, we find the most concentrated expression of what divine love should mean in the daily life of us, his followers.

Looking more closely at the text, we see that Jesus presents two themes, two dimensions of divine love; they are distinguished and yet intertwined. One theme is that the love of God is revealed and given to us in Jesus; the other that we should remain in his love and love one another as he loved us: love as gift and love as command. Both are inseparably connected. They are the center around which a life in Jesus forms itself.

"As the Father has loved me, so I have loved you."

"Love" is the core of Jesus' teaching; it should be the core of the life of anyone who claims to follow him. This does not mean that one should have realized this love perfectly, but that one is on the way, that one allows divine love to fashion life. Jesus' heart is filled to capacity with this message of love. To bring this message and to live it before our eyes he became incarnate. This message summarizes his mission. It breaks through in its fullness the moment he tries to communicate what moves him and what should move his disciples. Already this first verse manifests almost all that is essential in his message.

Later on Jesus gives us his commandment to remain in his love and to love one another. But, notice well, the commandment does not come first. First he announces the free and abundant gift of divine love to us; only then does he give the commandment to love in turn.

What is new in Christian life formation is not the commandment but the gift. The command to love is communicated already to Israel in the Hebrew scriptures. The newness of what Jesus brings is not so much centered in this commandment as in the revelation about the flow of divine formative love into our lives: "The love of God has been poured into our hearts by the Holy Spirit which has been given us." *(Rm.* 5:5)

Of what use would our mission to formative love be if we had not been blessed with a divine ability to love in the way Jesus asks us. The Gospel of St. John does not proclaim the commandment of love in the same manner as the Synoptic Gospels. St. John puts love-as-gift first, with an emphasis that cannot be mistaken. This does not mean that the commandment does not carry great weight in John. We shall see later how he will stress its significance. But he wants to impress on us that everything in the life of Christian formation should be based first of all on the insight that we would be unable to love if we were not loved first.

This primacy in the order of grace seems to parallel the primacy in the order of nature. We know that it is difficult, if not impossible, for people to really love others if they did not find any human love in their own life. In the order of grace even this human love experience is not sufficient. Our human ability to formative love has to be elevated to divine heights. This can only happen when the Holy Spirit grants us the transforming love of God himself.

St. John saved this message for the Last Discourse. Already the verse that introduces the washing of the feet of the disciples at this Last Supper points to this love: "Jesus knew that the hour had come for him to pass from this world to the Father. He had always loved those who were his in the world: but now he showed how perfect his love was." *(Jn.* 13:1)

The Last Discourse seems the best occasion for Jesus to tell his disciples how he loves them. In everyday life people don't usually tell their friends or pupils that they love them. They show it in the way they speak to them and deal with them. The disciples had often experienced the love of Jesus for them. Now at this solemn moment at the end of his life he puts words on their experience. Because of what they had felt in their contact with him, they are deeply touched by what he tries to say.

At the same time he reveals something to them about the interior life of the Holy Trinity: "As the Father has loved me, so I have loved you." *(Jn.* 15:9)

He takes their experience of his transforming love for them and elevates this awareness to an experience of what cannot be known or sensed by the human mind and heart alone.

This revelation of the mystery of the divine interforming love-life teaches us that the love of Jesus is not merely the overflowing of a tender heart. The love Jesus feels for us is the love of someone who has been sent. He loves as the One who must live before our eyes the transforming love of the Father. The same order of divine love applies to the Father: he loves the Son; everything else he loves in and through the Son. To understand divine love and its role in the Trinity and in our life, we must keep this order in mind.

What has been said in Chapter 14 and in the Prologue of this Gospel about seeing God is also true of loving God: "To have seen me is to have seen the Father." *(Jn.* 14:9) "No one has ever seen God; it is the only Son, who is nearest to his father's heart, who has made him known." *(Jn.* 1:18)

No one can fathom the meaning of "as the Father has loved me." It is a mystery in the eternal abyss of divinity. Our mind can never penetrate this unspeakable life of eternal interformative love. Many mystics and saints fell into silent ecstasy while contemplating this revelation of God's mysterious formation mystery. The only way in which we can approach a little of this forming love of God is by our presence in prayer to the incarnation of God in Jesus. In him we see the love of the Father indirectly as in a mirror. The only thing we can see in him directly is the love of the Son for the Father. We became aware of that love not so much when he speaks about his Father, but when he perseveres in obedience when the Father allows him to be handed over to the world.

When we meditate on this event we grow to the insight that the love of the Son must be immense, if he is willing to go through all of this suffering in total surrender. By the same token how great must be the love of the Father that it evokes such a response of love in the Son. This experience inspires the love of a person who has matured in the life of Christian formation. Anything we think and do in love is connected with the mission and the message of the Son and reaches to the trinitarian origin of his and our own life of formation.

A SHELL AROUND AN OYSTER

We thank you, Lord,
For your walking on this earth
As one of us.
You were a living message
Of forming love.
May your love be the center
Around which our life forms itself
Like a shell around an oyster
With its priceless pearl.
Melt all resistance
When your love begins to fashion
Our heart and its forming feeling.
Make us sense
The silent stream of love
That flows into humanity
From the mystery of the Trinity.

CHAPTER FIVE

"PLOUGHING, WE PRAISE;

SAILING, WE SING"
(Clement)

Remain in my love. If you keep my commandments you will remain in my love, just as I have kept my Father's commandments and remain in his love. I have told you this so that my own joy may be in you and your joy may be complete.

(Jn. 15:9-12)

Jesus tells us how our dwelling in his love gives shape and form to our daily existence. The history of our life is a history of formation. Plants and animals unfold in total subjection to the laws of nature. The laws of our development are far less detailed. As all human beings, I too am called by the Lord to give form in a wise way to my own spontaneous unfolding.

The burden of my life's formation rests upon me from birth to death. It is not instinct or drive but my spirit that guides this journey. Since the Fall our spirit is vulnerable; we need the healing Spirit of Jesus. He fortifies and deepens my spirit; my spirit is no longer the lonely shepherd of my life. Within it dwells the Spirit of Love: the Love between the Father and Jesus, the Love between him and me, the Love be-

tween me and others. When I dwell in this forming
Love, my life will be filled with joy.

The promise of Jesus is staggering. No matter
how wayward I am, he wants to infuse me with the
strength of his love, with its wholeheartedness, its
depth and fullness, its persistency in the face of
failure, its joy and resiliency.

The interformative love between the Father and
the Son is evident. Nothing could mar their oneness
or lessen the fullness of their communion. The unspeakable form of divinity is theirs in limitless perfection. The necessity of finite formation is human,
not divine. Even the humanity of our Lord was
subjected to the inevitability of finite formation that
marks all human life. But his formation — unlike
ours — could never veer away from the unfolding of
the life form the Father meant for him. He followed
graciously the directives the Father revealed to him.
They pointed to the mystery of his life direction. By
embracing them he grew slowly to his unique destiny.

No wonder the humanity of Jesus was loved by
the Father. But how can he love me similarly? My
path of life is soiled; it offends the pure Spirit of
Jesus. *Do two walk together unless they have agreed?*
(Amos 3:3) There is small agreement between Jesus'
Spirit and mine. And yet the transforming Love that
is the Spirit wants to be with me lastingly. The Lord
asks me to remain in that Love. For he knows it is the
only power that may transform my heart.

Jesus' spirit is a Spirit of compassion, dwelling in
me to save me from my deformities, to heal me and
make me whole. Jesus finds me lovable. He enriches
me with a source of love far beyond my human
powers. It cannot be compared with anything in this
life. Even Jesus himself is unable to describe it. He

can only compare it with the love of the Father's own heart for him. He gently invites me to hide in this love, not to shiver through life in the dead end streets of self fascination.

If you keep my commandments you will remain in my love, just as I have kept my Father's commandments and remain in his love.

Jesus' gift of love precedes his commands. Hence he can ask me to simply remain in a transforming love already given to me. By my own effort I could not work myself up to this love. It is his work alone. The only thing he asks of me is that I remain receptive, dwelling on his love in faithful attention, allowing it to form my life. Only this gift of love empowers me to keep his commandments.

Just as I have kept my Father's commandments and remain in his love. This *just as* is not a mere comparison between Jesus' and my way of love and obedience. It is infinitely deeper than that. My life and formation are meant to be absorbed in Jesus' own life and formation. Jesus' humanity enters my humanity. Yet I am not lost in this immersion. My distinctive destiny is miraculously enhanced. As the Canon says: *By the mystery of this water and wine may we come to share in the divinity of Christ who humbled himself to share in our humanity.* By his sharing in my humanity, I share in his divinity. I am assimilated in his affiliation with the Father.

In me and in fellow Christians, the love encounter of Father and Son is continued in time and space. The formative love of the Father engulfs my life. The Love that is the Spirit gives form to my unfolding. I become filled with Jesus' desire to do the Father's will, to disclose and follow his commandments. He does not speak here about the ten commandments; he means mainly the communications of transforming Love to my soul, inspiring life directives that are ever new, fresh, and vivid.

The daily channels the Spirit chooses to communicate life directives may seem dull to minds bent on the spectacular. Usually the Spirit speaks in the veiled language of the people, events and things that make up my life situation. He empowers me to see divine pointers in pedestrian events.

I have told you this so that my own joy may be in you and your joy may be complete. When I dwell daily in his forming love, when I feel embraced by his presence and share his affiliation with the Father, I am filled with joy. The fullness of Jesus' joy will touch my heart. Joy will be a graced disposition that slowly transforms my life. Such joy does not cancel out suffering and disappointment. They are less likely, however, to overwhelm my soul, to leave me in desperation. The Spirit will keep alive a flicker of light, a glimmer of joy in the midst of defeat. When the tempest is over, this glimmer will grow again to the fullness of joy Jesus intended for me.

I should not defraud myself of this gift by lack of response. Without joy my heart becomes grave and heavy, my life ponderous and dull. Filled with joy, no disappointment will deter me, no opposition halt my advance. Poise and composure will flow from the Lord's joy in the depths of my being.

Jesus' own life thrills with heavenly joy. He bears the good news that a new form of life can break through the gray formalities that imprison human existence. He announced it in the synagogue of Nazareth:

Unrolling the scroll he found the place where it is written: 'The Spirit of the Lord has been given to me, for he has anointed me. He has sent me to bring the good news to the poor, to proclaim liberty to captives and to the blind new sight, to set the downtrodden free, to proclaim the Lord's year of favor.' He then rolled up the scroll, gave it back to the assistant and sat down . . . Then he began to speak to them, 'This text is being fulfilled today even as you listen.'

(Lk. 4:16-21)

I am the homeless soul sheltered in tender care, the captive freed for a more open form of life in Jesus. I am the blind stumbler who receives the sight of a transcendent life direction. I am the downtrodden person, liberated by the vision of the Holy in the trivialities of everyday. Indeed the years of my life's formation shine forth as years of the Lord's favor.

Christ's formative presence in people can be traced by the joy he leaves behind. Where his Spirit is passing, sorrows are healed, desperation is lifted, tension is relieved, strained men and women are restored to peace. True Christians are joyful. The fruit of Christian formation is joy, a joy that enriches and amplifies my life. This joy is rooted in my sharing in my Lord's presence to the Father. It inspires me to spend myself in the service of humanity. The Lord's joy is a spring of dynamism filling my life with verve and elan where it might have been dismal and drab.

Each of us must experience this gift before we can begin to understand its power in human formation. It is not that the world changes and loses its dreary spots or that we shirk ugly events and repress the awareness of pain. Filled with the joy of Christ, I can allow myself to face darkness without fearing despair. By the power of the Spirit I can perceive reality without distortion. I can see mankind and its planet with all their ugliness but I can see also the hidden dimension that faith reveals. I can enjoy the final victory of the Lord over defeat and dreariness, a victory hidden in mystery but enfolding suffering humanity. The Spirit's gifts of faith, hope and love let light shine out of the darkness.

Christ's message of joy is proclaimed by the Church Fathers and early Christian writers. Clement exults, "All life has become a song." Elsewhere he adds, "Ploughing, we praise; sailing, we sing." Hermas calls the Holy Spirit, "A Spirit of Joy." Christians are described by Barnabas as, "The Children of Joy."

Our debt to these thinkers is incomparable, yet their splended tracts must be complemented by the vibrant message of the Gospel they explain. To return to the Gospel is like passing from the bracing highlands to the joyfulness of the valley teeming with life.

Perhaps I have dwelt onesidedly on Jesus as the man of sorrows and become forgetful of his joys. Maybe I did not allow the joyful Jesus of Nazareth, of the Resurrection, to form my heart. Nothing forms life more than the images I carry in my heart. If my only image of Jesus is that of the few hours he was hanging on the cross, I may fail to see the cheerful side of Christian life formation.

The image of the suffering Christ should be with me but also the joyous image of the graceful figure of the Lord as found in the etchings and icons of Eastern Christianity. His joy in life, his love of people, was so abundant that it scandalized the prim minds of the Pharisees. They denounce him as a wine drinker, a friend of sinners and publicans. Even in this last discourse, with betrayal and death closing in on him, Jesus could say: *I have told you this so that my own joy may be in you and your joy may be complete.*

PLOUGHING WE PRAISE; SAILING WE SING

Let me dwell daily in your love, my Lord;
Let it give gentle form to my unfolding.
Let me no longer be the lonely shepherd of my life.
Bring me home from the bracing highlands of the mind,
From the dead end streets in which I shiver in despair.
Shelter my soul tenderly when disappointment
*   hems me in.*
Do not allow my soul to grow ponderous and bleak,
Keep alive in me a glimmer of your joy,
Let no adversity deter my course,
No defeat my slow advance.
Put a spring in my step, a smile in my heart.
Let me spend this life lightheartedly.
Fill it with verve and inspiration.
Ploughing, we praise; sailing, we sing,
To land on the shore
That teems with your presence.

CHAPTER SIX

THE MYSTERY OF TRANSFORMING LOVE

This is my commandment:
love one another,
as I have loved you.
A man can have no greater love
than to lay down his life for his friends.
You are my friends,
if you do what I command you.
I shall not call you servants any more,
because a servant does not know
his master's business;
I call you friends,
because I have made known to you
everything I have learned from my Father.

(Jn. 15:12-16)

A friend is more than a comrade or an acquaintance. A friend guards you when you are off your guard, stays with you in trouble, does not forsake you when others let you down, restrains you from impetuosity, delights in your well being, shares in your saddness and grieves with you when life seems to turn against you. If necessary he will lay his life down for you. All human friendship pales in comparison with the friendship Jesus offers. He deepens human friendship as he deepens anything he touches.

He tells us that friendship implies a communication of one's deepest feeling and knowing: "I call you friends, because I have made known to you everything I have learned from my Father." *(Jn.* 15:15) The mysterious interiority of Jesus flows forth from the Father. All that he most deeply is he receives from the Father. Jesus as our friend makes us more and more share in these divine gifts.

Likewise, a good friend opens his heart and mind to the other, shares what he has learned, allows the other to know him as he really is.

Intimate communion, an unstinted sharing of one's interiority, is necessary in real friendship but not enough to prove its solidity. The test of friendship is the readiness to spend oneself for the other, even to give one's life if need be.

Real friendship is trust and loyalty. Christ's loyalty to us, our loyalty to him. He calls us to this intimacy. He wants us to be more than servants; we are to be his friends, to live with him in a wholehearted, spontaneous interformative relationship. In this interformation he assumes the active, we the receptive role. He forms us, his friends, first of all. But when we receive his forming friendship he calls us in turn to give uniquely form to his transformative presence in our history and culture. "I shall not call you servants any more . . . you are my friends . . . I call you friends." *(Jn.* 15:15) In no other person can we find the overflowing fullness of Christ's friendship. He keeps giving of himself to us, holding back nothing: "I have made known to you *everything* I have learned from my Father." *(Jn.* 15:15) He gives us the trust of a friend in spite of our failure to live up to it. "You did not choose me, no I chose you: and

I commissioned you to go out and to bear fruit, fruit
that will last." *(Jn.* 15:15) He chose me. He felt drawn
to me, his loved one. Since the Fall we are encased in
a counterfeit form of the divine life we are called to.
Our true form of life is the form, the image, the icon
of God in which we are created. Our counterfeit life
obscures the radiance of the divine form at the heart
of our humanity. Only a friend can bring out the true
me. The interformative love of a friend thaws the
counterfeit form in which I am frozen. Jesus is laying
down his life so that I may find mine. His caring
presence enables me to shed the old form to make
room for the unfolding of God's image in my life.

Jesus transforms first my interiority. He gives me
the grace of recollection. Like a caterpillar spins its
cocoon, so my Lord invites me to weave a sanctuary
of stillness around my wounded interiority. I may
look formless to others because I am losing my
counterfeit life with its make-believe exuberance. But
interiorly something new is forming because I am
called "friend" by Jesus in the depth of my soul. In
this sanctuary of silence he is making known to me all
he has received from his Father. The image of God in
me eventually breaks through the cocoon; the old
form is left behind. The new form of life in Jesus
unfolds and returns to the world, commissioned by
the Lord to go out and to bear fruit, fruit that will
last.

When the Father looks at the transformed me he
is delighted by his own image in Jesus. He cannot but
give anything I ask in the form, the name, the person
of Jesus. Asking in the person of Jesus is asking as
Jesus would ask. He would never ask anything that
displeases his father. Therefore, I should always add:
only if it is pleasing to you, my Lord.

The commission of the transformed me is first of all a commission of love. God is love. Any image of God in this world is a form of love. "This is my commandment: love one another, as I have loved you." *(Jn.* 15:12) "What I command you is to love one another." *(Jn.* 15:17) The friendship of Jesus becomes the mystical source of transforming friendship for others. A willingness to share in the forming love of the Trinity, to lay down our life for our friends bit by bit in daily service as the Lord laid down his life for us.

Pain and suffering, disappointment and failure, betrayal and misunderstanding are invitations of Jesus to seek the kingdom within. There he tells me: "I shall not call you servants any more, because a servant does not know his master's business." *(Jn.* 15:15) In the beginning I am hard of hearing: I am still too much tuned in to my counterfeit form of life. Not yet at home with my image of God I feel restless in the release from a form of living I have relied on for so long. A certain disorientation may depress me temporarily. Yet the transforming powers of the Trinity are stirring within. In the sanctuary of silence my divine form of life slowly awakens. Like the sleeping princess could be awakened only by the kiss of the prince, so my slumbering form of life is resurrected by the divine friend in my soul. I should gently surrender to the pace of the Spirit. A willful effort to hasten the process slows down the event of grace.

In God's own good time the bound up divine form will be released; it will be available to the unfolding of my life and the transformation of humanity. I can go out again to fulfill my life's commission. "Go out and bear fruit." *(Jn.* 15:16)

I shed my old way like and old skin. A new rhythm fills my life; divine vitality resonates in my spirit; my step becomes more firm; new responsibilities for the Church of Jesus are gladly assumed. A new form of life is born, a life in the image of God.

Before the transformation by Jesus' friendship we may not have been able to encounter all people in a respectful, loving way. We lived in the world, the house of God, as boarders not as loving members of his household. Estranged from the divine in our being, we developed a facility for keeping many at distance. A certain rigidness, stiffness, sometimes a negative, critical attitude made us a sign of discouragement instead of inspiration. If we cannot radiate respect and sympathy in our presence to people, we have not been transformed by the friendship of Jesus; we cannot bear fruit for them. As long as we are under the dominance of the counterfeit form of life, we lack warmth or restrict it only to a few in a possessive, exclusive way. We fail the command to love one another as I have loved you. The friendship of Jesus enables us to be compatible and comfortable with the wide spectrum of people we are called to bear fruit for. Without his friendship we feel vulnerable; we may become overdependent on a few people; we close ourselves off from others: we refuse to bear fruit for them.

If we refuse friendship our life may be comfortable but sterile and dried up, unencumbered by the demands that divine sympathy for people can make on our time and resources. Our personality flattens out; it is robbed of the depth which comes from embracing the sufferings of friendship that bearing fruit always entails. Our life becomes pointless. We miss out on God's marvelous design of transformation of people and world. It becomes difficult for us to approach others not in a possessive, manipulative, demanding way but respectfully in awe of the unique call of God in their life no matter how hidden and obscured. We operate from a repressed or denied image of God in us. Outside the friendship of Jesus our friendship for others dries up, suffocates and becomes impossible of fulfillment.

Jesus says to his disciples that they should love one another. That one another is first meant for the small, intimate group of disciples closed out by the world and its mundane pulsations. This circle of the few who remained faithful to him must be the beginning power of Jesus' transforming presence in the world. By loving one another they must make Jesus's love come to life in each other's heart. "Love one another as I have loved you." Because we love one another with his love, his love remains alive among us. Throughout this mystery of interformative love in Christ, a space for divine love is created in this world. This space is the Church. In the last discourse Jesus speaks not only to his disciples but to the whole Church.

St. John reformulated many words of Jesus in such a way that it would make sense not only to those who were with him in Israel but for all of us. The interior space of the Church is created by this interformative love in Jesus. It corresponds with the interiority of God in which the three divine persons are at one with one another in eternally forming love. This communion of formative love in God does not mean isolation. The world is not left to itself. The eternal formation of Father, Son and Spirit is the source of their forming presence in the world, their shared outer formation of universe, humanity and history.

When Jesus offers us his friendship he offers us to share in this eternal process of loving interformation at the heart of the Trinity. Similarly the interformative love of Jesus that is the heart of the Church does not mean isolation from humanity. The nourishing force of this love enables us to go out and to bear fruit in this world. Our fertility is rooted in the heart of the Church. The fruit, however, is not achievements that we can measure with a test of accountability. Fruits that truly form life are a mystery of availability to humanity. We never know for sure how many will eat and inwardly digest the fruit that the vine carries through us. We know only that if we try to keep the fruit for ourself it withers and decays. Only when we allow the fruit to be used up, either as nourishment or as a seed that falls in the earth and dies, will it be a leaven for humanity. Fruits will die on the vine if they stay too long. Giving them away will make room for ripe new fruits in our loving lives.

THE LIMPID TREASURE

You are the everlasting friend who holds me tenderly
In the palm of your wounded hand.
You share my sadness with a gentle smile.
You grieve with me in my distress,
You share with me a life laid down and spent,
You split apart the shell that encloses me,
The counterfeit form that is my life.
You lay bare the limpid treasure
At the bottom of my soul: the icon of the living God,
The miraculous form of life
That has been mine from all eternity.
Let me shed my old form like used up skin
And embrace the suffering that bearing fruit entails.
Let me, your worthless branch, bloom again.
Let me not wither and decay by holding back.

CHAPTER SEVEN

WITHDRAWN FROM THE WORLD

If the world hates you,
remember that it hated me before you.
If you belonged to the world,
the world would love you as its own;
but because you do not belong to the world,
because my choice withdrew you from the world,
therefore the world hates you.
Remember the words I said to you:
A servant is not greater than his master.
If they persecuted me,
they will persecute you too;
if they kept my word,
they will keep yours as well.
But it will be on my account that they will do all this,
because they do not know the one who sent me.
If I had not come,
if I had not spoken to them,
they would have been blameless;
but as it is they have no excuse for their sin.
Anyone who hates me hates my Father.
If I had not performed such works among them
as no one else has ever done,
they would be blameless;
but as it is, they have seen all this,
and still they hate both me and my Father.
But all this was only to fulfill the words written in
        their Law:

*They hated me for no reason.**
When the Advocate comes,
whom I shall send to you from the Father,
the Spirit of truth who issues from the Father,
he will be my witness.
And you too will be witnesses,
Because you have been with me from the outset.

(Jn. 15:18-27)
*Ps. 35:19

I have told you all this
so that your faith may not be shaken.
They will expell you from the synagogues,
and indeed the hour is coming
when anyone who kills you will think he is doing a
        holy duty for God.
They will do these things
because they have never known either the Father or
        myself.
But I have told you all this,
so that when the time for it comes
you may remember that I told you.

(Jn. 16:1-4)

"If the world hates you"

(Jn. 15:18)

John immortalized the sayings of Jesus for his Christians who suffered the resentment of many around them. They were ridiculed, persecuted and put to death for their faith. While remembering the words of Jesus he could not but be touched by this hate of Christians. John had lived through two generations of hostility against all who believed in the Name. All the meanness he had felt and seen during a long life must have become vivid for him when he wrote down words of Jesus foretelling the ill-will and the maliciousness his followers would have to bear with. Nobody remembers all the sayings of teachers deceased long ago, word by word, letter by letter. Neither did John. He had absorbed the core meaning of Jesus, communications during a life of loving contemplation. The Holy Spirit made sure that he would not distort the essential message; but in writing it down the aging apostle spelled these memories out in a way that would reach the heart of Christians who were suffering so much in their family and social life because they had given themselves wholeheartedly to the Lord.

His writing about the ill-will of others against Christians is meaningful for us too. If we really begin to form ourselves in the image of our Lord we cannot avoid displeasing others. Going against the false self that thwarts the emergence of the image of God in us we become, like Jesus, a sign of contradiction. Our attempt challenges the concerted effort of many people to form their personal and social lives in the image of an exalted humanity instead of the image of Jesus. Following him is experienced by them as a reproach, an unpleasant reminder.

Christ's own life evoked the same antagonism. It was foretold by the aged Simeon in the temple: "He is destined for the fall and the rising of many is Israel, destined to be a sign that is rejected . . . so that the secret thoughts of many may be laid bare." *(Luke* 2:34-35) When Jesus began his forming task among humanity by speaking his word he ran into resistance and vilification. The word of Jesus laid bare the exalted motivations and ambitions, the ruthless egoism of many: "[the world] does hate me, because I give evidence that its ways are evil." *(Jn.* 7:7-8) He could have said: because I *am* evidence that its ways are evil. The more a person emerges in the image or form of God the more his life and being makes many unwittingly aware that they are on the wrong path.

Few things are more resented by people than this kind of reminder. When we are children of a believing Christian family we are accustomed to be affirmed when we try to be good. We somehow expect the same to happen later in life. We never get totally over the fact that our attempts to be good may be met with suspicion, sarcasm, ridicule, anger and hostility. And yet that will unavoidably happen at times. It is a manifestation of the persecution Jesus predicts for all of us. After heartening us by promising his friendship, he warns about the troubles ahead of us. We will not be very popular no matter how nice we are. As true Christians we will be controversial. Of course, we may court opposition because of our small mindedness, fanaticism, intransigence and unflexibility. The then justified ill-will against us is not meant by Jesus when he speaks about hatred and persecution. He means the resentment evoked by our formation in the true image of Jesus.

If our Christian life formation never calls forth the dislike Jesus speaks about, we may ask ourselves if we are too compliant. Is our form of life perhaps less disquieting to the world than the Lord meant it to be? To be unpopular is unpleasant; it is better than to make no difference at all — better than to leave everyone at ease while human dignity is debased or denied. A Christianity that makes no difference is a false Christianity. What we are left with is a pale extraction of the original message of Jesus, a bland compromise between Christian and worldly formation.

"If you belonged to the world, the world would

love you as its own; but because you do not belong to the world, because my choice withdrew you from the world, therefore the world hates you." *(Jn.* 15:19) To be human is to be compelled to give some form to one's life, to one's spontaneous unfolding. Formation is always an interaction with a community. The community we allow to influence our formation begins to guide us in a profound way. Jesus mentions here first the community that forms us in the image of an exalted humanity alienated from the divine mystery of formation. He calls this community "the world." He opposes to it his own formative community. He tells us that we all are under the influence of worldly formation until he withdraws us by his choice from that merely secular community. He then goes on to tell us how the world he withdraws us from begins to hate us. Weak as we are we often fall back under the influence of the world. We have to be withdrawn by Jesus time and again. We should pray for this grace of divine withdrawal and for the strength to bear with derision if we do not conform any longer to the dictates of mere mundane pulsations. Some may listen to the word of Jesus that our very life speaks when we are faithful to him. Others will not. Their refusal may be due to ignorance, "because they do not know the one who sent me." *(Jn.* 15:21) Others are in a worse predicament that may become ours too: "If I had not come, if I had not spoken to them, they would have been blameless; but as it is they have no excuse for their sin. Anyone who hates me hates my Father. If I had not performed such works among them as no one else has ever done, they would be blameless; but as it is, they have seen all this, and still they hate both me and my Father. But all this was only to fulfill the words written in their Law: They hated me for no reason."

Already in Israel there were those who could have known. Their ignorance cannot be excused. They heard and saw Jesus, the word of life. Grace radiated from his very being, tried to touch their hearts but respected their freedom to refuse. Grace butted against a stone wall of indifference, prejudice and fear of the demands that following Jesus would entail. But the same can happen to us. To run into Jesus and his grace is a perilous thing. He is so eager to touch and transform our life. He calls forth the best in us. His light makes us see where we are wrong. To defend ourselves against that light we have to harden our hearts. Therefore, we pray in the holy office of the Church: "Today if we hear your voice let us not harden our hearts." The hardening of the heart means to put up excuses, rationalizations, constant criticisms, counter feelings that shelter us against the humbling insight into the truth of who we are. To resist so much light and power of grace we need more defenses and delusions than ever before in life. This hardening may stay with us for a lifetime. That explains why so many who were exposed in a special way to the forming power of the Lord in the Church, in a seminary or novitiate, in any other program of Christian formation may be worse off than before they received such unusual opportunities of graced formation. They could only escape its impact by using their time and energy to build frantically more escape hatches, defenses, rationalizations, complaints about what is *not* there. Without that special opportunity they would never have felt compelled to become so blinded against graced self-disclosure.

What was meant to be a period of grace becomes a period of damnation. Already during that period they may become an instrument of the evil one; they may try unwittingly to find support in their resistance by seducing others to share in their defensive negativity. They often win some over. The voice of the Holy Spirit is soft and not compelling, filled with respect for man's freedom to refuse the invitation of grace. The voice of the bad angel who speaks through these evaders of grace is loud and sharp, falsely pious, attractive and sometimes humorous. The spirit of evil has no concern about the freedom of people. It tries to trick and seduce them in every kind of way. Often he succeeds. Unfortunate are the people who later will be deformed in turn by those who proudly can say: "We went through a special period of formation; therefore we can help you." They do not tell the fearsome truth: "but we turned it into a place of deformation for ourselves. We hardened our hearts for a lifetime, we became arrogant men and women who speak not the humble language of Jesus but the proud language of worldly pulsations disguised as piety and formative wisdoms."

This mystery of iniquity at the heart of fallen humanity explains also that some former Christians are more entrenched in their hatred of Christ and his Church than those who never belonged to the community of Jesus. They have to be in order to keep their defenses against grace impenetrable. God keeps always calling them to his love. To muffle the divine invitation one has to expand constantly the inner forces of negativity. Of course, it is difficult to deny the goodness of the Infinite. Therefore, defensive negativity directs itself cunningly against the unavoidable limits of these who represent the Eternal word in our midst. It is the only way out. The terrifying truth is that some are the worse for the grace that comes their way through the imperfect representatives of Jesus.

By their refusal of surrender and defensive negativity they perverted the possibilities granted to them. This neglected grace will be the conclusive witness against them in the hour of judgment. Christ sorrowed for them. It pained him more than anything else: "If I had not come, if I had not spoken to them, they would have been blameless; but as it is they have no excuse for their sin." The sin of sins, the refusal of grace, the hardening of the heart by the evil of evils is found in constant negativity. Grace — that comes to us through limited human beings — also reveals to us what depth of humility and height of love God is calling us to; grace reveals to us the helps God offers us to rise to the invitation. Instead of surrendering to this grace we seek desperately for a way out. We focus critically on the imperfections of those who have been called by him to pass on his message. We claim that we are called to improve them but in fact we shrink back from the painful self-knowledge they summon us to. We do not want to take what God puts in our reach through them. We turn our backs upon the graced opportunities presented to us. Our failure in formation is now a far worse failure, our doom a darker doom.

"If I had not performed such works among them as no one else has ever done, they would be blameless; but as it is, they have seen all this, and still hate both me and my Father." When we share with others a period or a community of graced formation we cannot escape the experience that Jesus works in the souls of those among us who surrender to the opportunity, that he forms them in humility and truth as no one else has ever done. There are moments in which we ourselves let up on our negativity sufficiently to experience in our own life the forming presence of Jesus, who calls himself meek and humble of heart. In spite of these works of grace we resume our refusal to surrender under the pretext of the imperfections of his messengers. This is worse than our wrongdoings before this period of graced formation. Then we may have failed because we did not know as well the hand he extended to us. Now we have seen in our own life and that of others that in him we can rise above our negativity, our defensive need to belittle and detract. By knowingly refusing the special grace of formation granted to us, our end is worse than our beginning. Never again can things be with us the way they were before we entered a privileged period, community or program of graced formation.

THE ARROGANCE OF THE ELECT

How many hate your name?
Who is to blame
For such hostility?
Is it the futility
Of Christian formation?
Where is the consecration
Of the sweet wine
Of compassion, the sign
Of your presence, reverently?
They pass indifferently,
With the arrogance of the elect,
While they wrecked,
Instead of blessed
The dream of the oppressed
For a home of their own
Beyond the steel and chrome
Of the loveless city
That shows no pity;
That kills the mind
With its grind
Of bureaucratic pressure,
That dims the light
And dulls the fight
Against levelling
Of everything.
Rescue them,
From the pen
Of uniformity,
Cattle dazed
Debased and raised
For profit only.
Oppressors are displeased
Because we never ceased
To praise your liberating name,
Reminding them of the stain
Of justice denied
To all who cried and died
In the night of neglect
By the lofty elect.

CHAPTER EIGHT

WITNESS BY APPEAL

When the Advocate comes, whom I shall send to you from the Father, the Spirit of Truth who issues from the Father, he will be my witness and you too will be witnesses, because you have been with me from the outset. *(Jn.* 15:26-27)

A new thought emerges here in Jesus' last discourse. He speaks about being a witness. This invitation to witness is new at this supper conversation; it is not new in the Gospel of John. This Gospel more than the others highlights the witness aspect of our life.

Already in the prologue the Evangelist describes the life of John the Baptist as a witnessing for the Light. *(Jn.* 1:7) The more we allow our unique life form to emerge, the more we become transformed into divine light. This light that we are in the Lord cannot but manifest itself in our daily ways. We radiate him, we become witnesses by our very being.

Speaking to his disciples Jesus knows that he will rise in glory, that he will be an ongoing manifestation of light in this world, that he will send the Spirit of Truth to dwell in humanity as never before. Those who will be faithful to his word, to his kingdom, to his presence will "see" him; they will experience the risen Lord in their hearts. Their very being will become a proclamation of the good news. The good news is that we can now discover and realize in Christ the unique image of God in us that we are invited to unveil. Our enlightened life will witness also that creation itself can be transfigured by people who are transformed themselves by the Spirit of Jesus. "Go into the whole world and proclaim the good news to all creation." *(Mk.* 16:15)

Proclaiming the good news to others cannot mean imposing the news upon them. Neither can true formation in the Lord be a result of clever propaganda. The Spirit of Truth does not transform people by slick advertisement or coercion, by brainwashing or seduction. The Spirit in us evokes faith in our witness by gentle appeal to their spirit. There is nothing coercive about our modes of appeal. They can be resisted, denied and ridiculed. An appeal spares the freedom of others to evade the divine invitation that our witness should be. It leaves them enough space to rationalize our witness away. God wants only hearts that freely surrender to the luminous form of life he draws them to silently. Jesus himself experienced how his own apostles were unable to allow themselves to be touched by the faith of those who had seen him in his risen presence. "He took them to task for their disbelief and their resistance, since they had put no faith in those who had seen him after he had been raised." *(Mk.* 16:14) We too, as witnesses for the Lord, will meet this disbelief and resistance. It is painful to be an appeal that is bypassed in indifference — worse if it is resisted stubbornly or demeaned maliciously.

Why do people turn against the witness of a life that points to the possibility of resurrection? Because it is a threat. To allow one's heart to be opened even slightly to the witness of the Spirit is to risk being invited to a transformation that touches all of one's life. To prevent this risk the defenses against formative grace have to be expanded and strengthened in any thinkable way. The heart becomes a fortification, immune to any inspiration. This person is worse off after meeting the witness than before. His receptivity may have been diminished dangerously because of anxious increase in deformative security directives that seem almost demonic.

To be formed into the image of Jesus means thus also to be formed into a witness. Jesus himself says: "I was born for this, I came into the world for this; to bear witness to the truth." *(Jn.* 18:37)

People cannot directly behold the light that is the presence of the Lord in history. The light of his presence has to be fractured through the manifold unique forms that our lives take on in this world. Each of us is called to his own journey from the land of darkness to the land of likeness with the light. The light of truth can be seen only with the eyes of faith. It is a faith in things unseen. God uses the witness of each unique form of life to evoke that faith in others.

People do not see Jesus with their own eyes, hear him with their own ears, touch him with their own hands. The apostles have seen, heard and touched him. They are the witnesses for what they experienced directly in their immediate presence to Jesus. Precisely for that reason he had chosen and appointed them. Therefore he says here: "And you too will be my witnesses, because you have been with me from the outset."

It is true that these original witnesses are no longer alive. Yet their witness is still the foundation of our faith today. The Church inherited their witness. Over centuries and cultures the Church passes their witness on to us through her messengers. They proclaim the message on basis of the divine power of their office. This official proclamation has to be complemented by the witness of the increase of all of us in the image of the Lord. Our witness incarnates the official witness of the Church in this world. It is this miracle of the enfleshment of Jesus in each believer that touches humanity everywhere. Each Christian is responsible for his own little corner where God has placed him in time and space. His witness there has to be unique, first in terms of the people he is called to serve, secondly in terms of the divine likeness he is invited to by his Baptism as this one irreplacable Christian. I should be deeply convinced that there will never be another Christian at any other time or place in history who will have the same life call as I. Nobody else will ever be born who can be a witness in the same way as I.

One way of witnessing is witnessing by words. The impact of these words can be very different. Their weight depends on the life that sustains and validates them. Our words of witness are usually not more influential than our life. The witness of the apostles gained immensely in power because all of them sealed it with their blood. They gave their lives for it. The same was true of the witness of Jesus. His passion and death affirmed strikingly the words he had spoken, his claim to be sent by the Father. We too have to give our life in service of the witness we bring to people. Few of us will be called to sacrifice our life in martyrdom. All of us are invited to lay that life down little by little. Our new form in Christ demands that we die to the old one that was a counterfeit. The old form was narrow and self-centered. We did not care much for others. In the new form of life we allow the Spirit to work in us as the Spirit of Truth. He reveals to us the truth of God's loving presence in all persons. The awareness that each of them is called to unfold their unique life in Christ evokes our respect and care for all. The Spirit of Truth moves us to lay our life down bit by bit in our daily attempt to foster and facilitate their unique formation in the Lord.

This gift of our life validates out witness in their eyes more than anything we ever say. Of course, we should not misunderstand this gift as blindly giving in to anything people desire. Neither should we in the name of love protect people against the formative power of reality. For example, there exists today an organization of family members who have to cope with a father, mother or child who suffers from alcoholism. The first thing these people learn is to grow unselfishly in what is sometimes called "tough love." They are made to realize that the worst and most unkind thing they did to alcoholics was to rob them of the formative lessons of reality. They protected them against losing face in daily life. They made excuses for them, sometimes to themselves and sometimes to others. They covered their absences and mistakes. They did not allow them the beneficial, formative lesson of failure. In all these ways their lack of real love made it impossible for alcoholics to be confronted with the consequences of their deforming illness and to seek help in the appropriate places.

Are we not all similarly afraid to witness for formative love? We are scared of the dislike we may suffer if we engage in real love. We fear the discomfort formative love may create in our cozy lives. Instead of tough love that forms us realistically, we settle for its sentimental surrogate. Behind a veil of sweet understanding we protect our own popularity while we allow people to destroy themselves. We allow a husband, wife, child, student, community member, employer or employee to get away with self-deception. We prevent this person from experiencing the grace of discipline that flows from reality if we transgress against it. Sentimental fathers and mothers, weak superiors, and soft teachers have destroyed the lives of many. They shielded them unwisely against the formative teachings of reality.

To allow God to speak in daily reality is only one way of formative love that witnesses for God's presence. Sometimes we are called to witness in words. We can only give the right word if we give with that word also ourselves. This was the way in which the apostle Paul experienced his being a witness. He tells us about this in the first document that we have about Christian witnessing, Paul's first letter to the Thessalonians. He assures us there:

> We constantly thank God for you that as soon as you heard the message that we brought you as God's message, you accepted it for what it really is, God's message and not some human thinking; and it is still a living power among you who believe it.
>
> (1 *Th.* 2:13-14)

In the same letter he proclaims the gift of himself that went with the gift of the word: "Like a mother feeding and looking after her own children, we felt so devoted and protective towards you, and had come to love you so much, that we were eager to hand over to you not only the Good News but our whole lives as well.

Let me remind you brothers, how hard we used to work, slaving night and day so as not to be a burden on any one of you while we were proclaiming God's Good News to you. You are witnesses, and so is God that our treatment of you, since you became believers, has been impeccably right and fair. You can remember how we treated everyone of you as a father treats his children, teaching you what was right, encouraging you and appealing to you to live a life worthy of God who is calling you to share the glory of his Kingdom." (1 *Thess.* 2:8-12)

Paul underwrote his witness with the gift of himself that made it possible for the Thessalonians to hear the message of God in Paul's appealing words. Paul was not a witness of Jesus in the historical sense. He did not accompany Jesus on his long travels through Galilee. He did not hear him personally nor did he see his miracles with his own eyes. He did not witness directly the passion and crucifixion of our Lord. Whatever he knew about these events came to him in two ways, as it comes to us. Jesus revealed himself to Paul in his own heart through the Holy Spirit. The second revelation came by his obedient entrance into the formation tradition of the first apostles.

The witnessing of St. Paul is an important example for us. We too are sharers in his situation. We did not experience a direct encounter with the Lord, but like him we too have to witness for what is given to us by the apostles and their successors. We too have to be witnesses touched deeply by the Holy Spirit. Finally, what we say as witnesses for the Church must pass through our personal experience.

LIKE A STAINED GLASS WINDOW

Thank you for the invasion of your Spirit
Who makes us a witness of your light,
Your journey through humanity,
The living proclamation of a mystery
That transfigures earth invisibly.
Let us not betray your forming presence
By propaganda, seduction, brainwashing
Or coercion of simple, anxious souls.
You want the witness of gentle appeal
That leaves each person free to surrender or to resist
Your invitation to a luminous form of risen life.
Let our life remain an appeal to faith
Even if they bypass us, indifferent and cold.
Make us understand in compassion
Why the human heart became a fortification
Against your work and the witnessing we ought to do.
In spite of unworthiness let our lives
Fracture the soft light of your presence
Like a stained glass window filters
The radiance of the sun in countless colors.
Make us light up uniquely the corner of the universe
Where we are placed in time and space
Like candles in a dark and empty hall,
Laying down our life little by little
In service of all who pass our way in history.
Let our love be strong and honest
Never a refuge from reality and suffering,
Not sentimental but impeccably right and fair,
So that not we, but you may rise in the heart
Of the multitudes in search of
A shepherd for their lives.

CHAPTER NINE

INTREPID ADVENTURERS IN
THE LAND OF FORMATION

I have told you all this so that your faith may not be
shaken. But I have told you all this, so that when the
time for it comes you may remember that I told you.

(Jn. 16:1-4)

Only now does Jesus tell his disciples in painful
detail what the hatred of some people will do to them;
they will be banned from the synagogues, even
brought to death. As long as he was with them it had
not been necessary to prepare his simple unsuspecting
friends for such calamities. But now he tells them so
that they may remember in moments of persecution;
it should strengthen their faith: I have told you all this
so that your faith may not be shaken.

*Lord, your sensitivity for the readiness of your
friends tells us how considerate you are with all of us.
You are the mystery of formation in our life. How
gentle you are in the unveiling of that mystery. You
adapt the pace of your inspirations to the pace of our
unfolding. Your ongoing formation of our life reveals
itself bit by bit, here a little and there a little. Your*

formative inspiration is a timely response to our readiness to receive. The more we grow confident in your presence the more you reveal to us the secrets of our life form, the image of God each of us must find in you. You make us see the divine formation we have to go through with its promises and demands, its joys and sufferings.

You are too loving to overwhelm us with an avalanche of directives we cannot yet assimilate. You are never premature in the direction of our life. Neither do you want us to be staggered by misunderstanding because we would not be prepared to expect misunderstanding as a fact of life. Like the apostles you want us to be aware that suffering and misunderstanding will be our part if we try to realize your form of life in this world.

Formation in Christ is a gradual and gentle unfolding of baptismal grace; a wading deeper and deeper into the mystery of our always ongoing divine formation. To be formed in Christ ought to mean that every new life situation opens up new horizons. To accept our baptismal call to formation in Christ is only a point of departure. We must grow from life form to life form, from grace to grace.

Each new current form of life must be a richer, more mature response in Jesus to the new providential situation that evokes this response. Each change must bring us nearer to the unique image of God meant for us from eternity until we reach our full stature in Jesus that Saint Paul speaks about. Life as it passes ought to be deepening our vision of the divine image that should be ours in him. This vision enables us to see far more meaning in our personal history than we initially do. Our faith in the formative power of all events is deepened. It strengthens our resolve to cope gently with the pains and problems that may besiege us in new periods of formation.

Often new trenches have to be cut in new situations. We are better able to do so if we believe that the Spirit of Jesus is leading us on. We must be ready for new enlightenments because Christ — as he said to his apostles — has still many things to tell us, but we cannot bear them yet. Our unique life form in Jesus has to grow, expand and mature; it is only slowly, and step by step, that we disclose and realize our divine image.

At first, we may only follow Christ in holy fear. Then we may gain some peace and comfort in a growing awareness of Christ's formative love for us. No longer are we driven mainly by fear in our task of formation but more by a feeling of duty to perform as well as we can for his sake. Functional ambition has replaced vital anxiety. We want to do the right thing at the right time in the right way. Finally, the Lord may allow us the experience of loving union with the one whose image is at the core of our personality. This union hastens the attainment of the unique image of God we are to find and express in our life. The divine form disclosed to us in the end is much richer, fuller and truer than we could expect in the beginning of our journey.

But this presupposes that we are intrepid adventurers in the land of formation. Some of us pitch our tent too early, settling down in one limited, current form of presence to reality. We do not go beyond the initial gift of divine formation. We do not venture out into the new meanings a new life situation may yield; and so we never discover the new possibilities of formation in Christ that lie waiting for us, that should be ours. We do not allow ourselves to feel the invitation of God's deeper plan for us, with its unexpected horizons of growth in Jesus.

Horizons of divine formation keep receding as we approach them, attracting us on and on. That is true not only of us personally, but also of the journey of Christianity through the centuries. Range rises behind range, and peak towers above peak in the formative self-manifestation of Christ in history. What any community, culture, or cultural period can express in its own unique image of Christ is a mere segment of his fullness as the image of God. In the thought of St. Paul it takes the forms of all saintly lives and cultures — the particular angles of the richness of Christ they represent — to give us an inkling of what Christ is as the Eternal Image or Form of the Godhead.

> I did not tell you this from the outset, because I was with you; but now I am going to the one who sent me. Not one of you has asked, "Where are you going?" Yet you are sad at heart because I have told you this. Still I must tell you the truth; it is for your own good that I am going because unless I go, the Advocate will not come to you; but if I do go, I will send them to you.   *(Jn.* 16:4-7)

The going away of Jesus is not the topic of the last discourse. Yet it is the event out of which all topics of this discourse blossom forth. It is the theme out of which ever new themes are built up, the occasion that opens us up again and again to new insights in the meaning of our formation in between our Lord's departure and his return to us.

In this text Jesus develops another meaningful aspect of this event: "I am going — but . . . it is for your own good that I am going because unless I go, the Advocate will not come to you." The Spirit

cannot come to assist the disciples in their formation
while Jesus himself is still with them as the divine
image their life should grow to. The two divine
guides of life's unfolding will not both assist them
on earth at the same time. The formation of the
disciples will benefit from the leaving of the Master
in spite of their sorrow. His lasting visible presence
would delay their acceptance of full responsibility for
their own formation. They would count too much on
him to settle their problems and to solve their crises
of transcendence.

The formative presence of Jesus must become
interiorized in a unique way by each disciple to leave
him with a new sense of responsibility. Their faith too
will mature when his presence is no longer tangible
and obvious. They will have to mature in faith while
moving forward in a world of shadows. Yet, it is for
their own good that he is going.

Before this promise of the Spirit Jesus seems to
reproach his disciples: "Not one of you has asked,
'Where are you going?' Yet already Peter (13,36) and
then Thomas (14,5) did ask him this question. These
words of Jesus are not meant as a reproach. They are
an invitation to reflection. You have asked the right
questions with the wrong attitude. Therefore my
answer could not touch and transform your heart.
You are so caught in your fantasies about me, your
own fears, exalted ambitions and expectations that
you cannot ask the question as it should be. Because
you do know neither the depth of the question nor the
depth of the answer. You do not realize that my
leaving will benefit your life. Therefore "you are sad
at heart because I have told you this." It is only then
that Jesus tried to tell them that it is for their own
good that he is going and that it will make free the

way for the Holy Spirit he will send to them.

Jesus' simple expression "going" really means his sacrificial death. The fruit of the sacrifice of Jesus is the Holy Spirit. The Divine Counselor is only given to humanity through the gift of Jesus' life. He is the great farewell gift of the Lord. The Holy Spirit is the utmost self communication of God. This infusion of the Spirit must first find form in one obedient human being before he could be infused in many as a principle of divine formation. St. Irenaeus says it strikingly: "The Holy Spirit needed to get used to abide in people by abiding first in Jesus."

The son of God had allowed the Spirit of God to give form to his human life. Dying, he brought the formation of his humanity to a close in this Spirit. This closure merited the abiding of the Spirit in all who would seek their life form in Jesus. The Divine Counselor will direct each follower uniquely to represent and complement in his life some aspect of the form he realized in Jesus' humanity. Elsewhere the Evangelist explains why the Spirit was not yet formative in the followers of Jesus during his life on earth: "because Jesus was not yet glorified." *(Jn.* 7:39)

> And when he comes, he will show the world how wrong it was, about sin, and about who was in the right, and about judgment: about sin: proved by their refusal to believe in me; about who was in the right: proved by my going to the Father and your seeing me no more; about judgment: proved by the prince of this world being already condemned. *(Jn.* 16:8-11)

The Counselor is more than the formative light in the heart of the faithful. On his arrival he will also attack the counter formation of the world, whose prince is Satan. On three counts will he show the wrongness of worldly formation and reverse its erroneous impact on those who believe in Jesus. He will show the sinfulness of a formation aiming at conformity to a mere human image of perfection while rejecting the formative image of Christ through unbelief and blindness, pride and prejudice.

Christ's life as a formative image for humanity may have seemed discredited by his death on the cross. But the ongoing power of the Spirit in history will evidence that he was in the right. His death was not an end but a beginning: returning to the Father the reign of graced formation has begun. Welcomed by the Father as "the Holy and Righteous One" his formative power begins to spread through humanity. *(Acts* 3:14, 2:36, 5:30-32) In this light the prince of deformation stands already condemned: it will become increasingly clear how the invisible sources of deformation in this world have overreached themselves in crucifying the Lord of glory. *(Jn.* 12:31; 14:30; I *Cor.)* John, the visionary of Patmos saw the fall of the prince of deformation in many visions. *(Apoc.* 12:9; 20:2; 2:8)

Also in this sense "it is for your own good that I am going." On earth, it was in the main merely a local formative influence Jesus could exert; whereas now, he is formatively present in the Spirit, the whole world over. Wherever we may be we can be instantly face to face with the Lord of glory. His form grows in history. We enter into the fruit of the formative toil, thought and faith of those who followed the Counselor's inspiration before us. This enables us to give richer form to the risen and rising life of Christ in history. Neither can we assume that our generation will plumb the depths of Christ, the Image of God. Later generations looking back at us will wonder how we failed to find in him a beauty of form that will be obvious to them by then. For each age and culture as it passes is meant not only to give form to what has been grasped before, but to disclose new formative dimensions in this inexhaustible image of God that is Christ. These we have to hand on as henceforward part of our formation tradition. New astonishments will keep breaking in on humanity while participating in the divine mystery of formation that carries its own ongoing history.

In the spiritual formation of any people, or any civilization, the struggle between formation and deformation continues. The discussion takes place on various levels of the culture. The discussion on the highest levels can be of the greatest influence. The formative directives these levels disclose and propagate will sink down into the daily life of the simple and the economically poor.

Unfortunately the souls of many cultural leaders in our civilization seem empty and abandoned; their spiritual poverty can be immense; pride and sophistication may have entrenched them in a vacuum of faith. To serve the formative power of the Spirit in those abandoned higher walks of life is a heavy duty of Christianity. It is most difficult for the Church to find able and dedicated workers — even among clergy and religious — for this despised and thorny corner of the vineyard. The missionary of the sophisticated may have to forego for a lifetime the consolation and warm affirmation that the simple and economically poor often grant their spiritual leaders, especially when they promise to enhance also their material situation. Especially celibate leaders may unconsciously yearn for this warm attachment of simple followers. We may be tempted to look down upon the few among us who are condemned to spend their life in this less rewarding, inconspicuous, somewhat lonely apostolate of cultural discussion and creation. Yet if they would leave the most abandoned in the leading walks of life also the less abandoned among the simple would suffer. They would be harmed in the long run. We would condemn their children to be victimized by a civilization that because of our absence will be formed outside the Christian tradition.

It will become a culture with little peace and justice for all on all levels of life. In such a culture it is difficult to survive as a transcendent and inspired person. Christian thinkers, writers, artists, scholars and scientists are called to participate in the Spirit's judgment or appraisal of cultural formation. In the light of Christian directives (or appraisal) they must measure cultural directives. They must indicate how Christ can assume a new form in their civilization. All Christians ought to facilitate the lonely apostolate among the most abandoned and spiritually poor dimensions of the culture those few are called to. We should create the right conditions for their study and their labors. Even if we are unable to appreciate their works and to profit from them personally, we should deeply respect their difficult calling and support their participation in the appraisal of the Spirit by our prayers.

INTO A VIRGIN LAND

You wait my Lord
Not wanting to distort
The pace of my unfolding.
Your withholding
Of the mystery
Of my destiny,
The secret of the journey
That is to be
Into a virgin land
Unknown and yet at hand
Concealed in the events
In which I spend
My daily life.
Beyond its din and strife,
Its polluted streams,
The songs of the sirens
Are calling me
To simply be
In hope and belief,
In readiness to receive
Your inspiration,
The penetration
Of your presence
Already speaking in events
That bind my days together.
You call me gently
To the land of transformation
Where destination
Is shrouded
Beyond horizons
That daily recede
And impede
Exalted manipulation
In anxious concentration
On projects of human pride.
Your mystery is a tide
That sweeps me along
Until I belong
To you alone
And freely roam
In the desert of unknowing.

CHAPTER TEN

A CHALICE WAITING
TO BE FILLED WITH LIGHT

I still have many things to say to you
but they would be too much for you now.
But when the Spirit of truth comes
he will lead you to the complete truth,
since he will not be speaking as from himself
but will say only what he has learned;
and he will tell you of the things to come.
He will glorify me,
since all he tells you will be taken from what is mine.
Everything the Father has is mine;
that is why I said:
All he tells you
will be taken from what is mine.

(Jn. 16:12-15)

Jesus insists that the words and deeds that touched so deeply the lives of his friends are not coming from himself alone. All transformation comes from the Father. His formation of his friends has been a tender sharing of what he has heard from Him. *(Jn.* 15:15) Yet they were not yet ready for it. *(Cf. I Cor.* 3:1-2) Their formation must be continued by the Spirit of Truth until they can receive their unique life form in Christ in its fullness. The Spirit's formative power will be the same as that on which Jesus had relied in his formative presence to his disciples. *(Jn.* 3:32; 7:16-17; 8:26; 12:49; 14:10) The Spirit's formation will continue the formative direction of Jesus, *"since all he tells you will be taken from what is mine."* In doing so *"He will glorify me."*

Jesus' words and works allowed the glory of the Father to shine forth. *(Jn.* 12:28) They revealed the nature and the splendid purpose of the ongoing divine formation of world, humanity and history. Similarly, the glory of the Son's formative power in history *(Jn.* 11:4; 12:23; 13:31) will be experienced more fully after his earthly, bodily passage through this world. The transformative impact of the Pneuma will manifest gradually the healing influence of Jesus on this planet and its history.

Jesus had already declared that his passion and death are the supreme manifestation of the obedience to the Father's will that formed his life to the end. They are the climax of the divine formation of his human life. That truth has yet to be fully grasped by his friends. Only when they understand it deeply in their hearts will they be able to participate fully in the obedient formative presence of Jesus among us. The Spirit will continue and complete the unfinished formation not only of the twelve but of all of us until the end of time. Yet one more formative task of the Spirit is to be announced: *"he will tell you of the things to come."*

Our life is formed by anticipations. We live by what we hope to happen to us. The Spirit of Christ is the Spirit of transcendent anticipations. He will remind us of the ultimate form the body of Christ to which we belong will attain in eternity. He will inspire us with the anticipation of the Lamb seated upon the throne, surrounded by all of us in glory. *(Cf. Rev. 4:1-11; 5:12-13; 19:10; 22:3).*

What Jesus stresses here are the richness, the benefits, the depths our lives will gain because of the other Helper he will send. In foregoing sentences Jesus directed the disciples' reflection to their struggle in the world, the form they would have to give to history, the sufferings implied in that task. Here their attention is redirected to their own formation. Jesus touches on the mystery of the inner formation of the three divine Persons in the Godhead and the inner formation of the disciples. Both mysteries are inter-twined.

"I still have many things to say to you but they would be too much for you now." Our true form of life is an open form. We must form our life in such a way that it becomes a total openness to God. This unconditional opening of our life to the Divine readies us for a transformation only he can bring about. The open life form may be symbolized as a lily opening up to the sun or a chalice waiting to be filled to the brim. The Divine is such an immense reality that its revelation is too much for us when we have not been raised beyond our infancy in the life of the Spirit.

The psalmist tries to express the overwhelming experience when God begins to fill the life that has become an open chalice for Him.

> The floods lift up, O Lord,
> the floods lift up their voice:
> the floods lift up their tumult.
> More powerful than the roar of many waters.
> more powerful than the breakers of the sea —
> powerful on high is the Lord.   *(Ps. 93:3-4)*

And yet the same powerful Presence is deeply desired
by the person who has attained the open form of life.

> Whom else have I in heaven?
> And when I am with you, the earth delights me not.
> Though my flesh and my heart waste away,
> God is the rock of my heart and my portion forever.
> For indeed, they who withdraw from you perish;
> you destroy everyone who is unfaithful to you.
> But for me to be near God is my good.

(Ps. 73:23-28)

How can we dwell in God's presence as open
flowers in a burning sun without withering away in
the rays of his immensity? We have to be formed in
this tolerance of the Infinite. This can be done only by
a divine director, who is at home in the Infinite and
dwelling within us. The third Person of the Trinity is
that director. *"But when the Spirit of truth comes he
will lead you to the full truth."*
    "Truth" in the writings of St. John is the fullness
of God's reality desiring to communicate itself to us.
Leading us to the fullness of truth is the finest act of
formation by the Pneuma in the center of our being.
This art of final formation, of step by step initiation
into a life form that opens up fully to the Divine, is
the art of arts attributed to the Spirit. This art of the
Spirit ties in well with the promise of Jesus:

> but the Advocate, the Holy Spirit,
> whom the Father will send in my name,
> will teach you everything
> and remind you of all I have said to you.

(Jn. 14:26)

One dimension of the sublime formation by the
Spirit is to help us make our own the words of Jesus

that remain too much outside our heart. This interior formation by the words of Jesus opens us step by step to the truth which is the fullness of Divine Reality. Then the Holy Spirit guides us into the fullness of the truth, which we could never enter without his guidance: *"since he will not be speaking as from himself but will say only what he has learned."*

Jesus clarifies what is meant by the "full truth." We have seen that it is the fullness of God's reality. But the fullness of the Divine is the fullness of God's Trinitarian life. The Spirit of Truth's final formation of our life is the initiation into the mystery of ongoing formation within the Holy Trinity. The Three Divine Persons make each other be from eternity. We call this eternal Event, without beginning, change or end, formation in an analogical sense. Our interformation here on earth is a shadow of the mystery of divine interformation. Our formation is a finite changing process; the intra- and inter- formation of the Trinity is an eternal Event. In this formative event the three Divine Persons form each other from eternity as Three Persons and yet form together the perfect community of only one God.

Our formation is meant to participate in that mystery of divine formation. The Holy Spirit initiates us into the formation Event of the Trinity in the measure that we grow into our unique image in Christ. The Father and the Spirit are forming us in Jesus. In that sense we are participants in the formation Event of the Trinity.

The Holy Spirit speaks to our heart only what he has learned; he will form our interiority by communicating to our soul what flows forth from this interformation of the Divine Persons. The event of eternally ongoing formation within the Trinity is the highest interior exchange within the Godhead. This formation Event constitutes the essence of the Trinitarian life. It is an exchange of life. If it were possible in God, it would imply an increase of life.

Our interformation within the human community resembles somewhat this formation Event. We experience a disclosure and deepening of our emergent form of life when a loving person affirms our becoming. He may, moreover, enrich our formation by communication of riches of life found by fidelity to his own style of emergence. He or she evokes formative potencies in us we may not have known existed in us. Or, if we knew of them, they begin to mean more for us because of the formative, affirmative presence of the other. Such formative presence makes our own form of life deeper, richer, more glorious.

"He will glorify me, since all he tells you will be taken from what is mine." The hidden form of Jesus is already in us; it participates in the formation Event of the Trinity. The formative presence of the Holy Spirit will disclose to us our unique image in Christ. Only then will we begin to surmise our potentialities and the divine glory that is ours that has to shine forth gradually in all the dimensions of our day to day life.

And what is this hidden form of God in us? We could say: it is the unique form or image of the whole, living fullness of God in each person. "Everything the Father has is mine; that is why I said: All he tells you will be taken from what is mine."

We grasp now a little the mystery of the formation Event within the Trinity and of the participation of our formation process in that Event. The Father as formative Origin is the fullness of Divinity. Yet also the Son because of his eternal formation by the Father possesses *"the complete truth"* of divinity.

His Godhead is personalized, however, by the unique life form of Sonship. This truth of the life form of the Son is not immediately disclosed to us in its fullness. This disclosure is the mission of the Holy Spirit, who is formed eternally by the formative interaction of Father and Son. Jesus calls him, therefore, the *"Spirit of truth."* He is the One through whom the truth of God's and our formation and their graced intertwining becomes communicable. Through him the formative interaction between Father and Son is passed on to us. He draws our formation process into the divine formation Event. As St. Paul says,

"you are filled with the utter fullness of God."

(Ep. 3:19)

All formation finds its ultimate origin in the Father through whom all that exists received its form. It is achieved in the Son who resides in our hearts through faith and inspired knowledge. The realization of this origination in the Father and of this achievement of our form in the Son becomes possible through the Holy Spirit. In this way the richness of God's glory finds form in us, filling us with the fullness of his truth.

RADIANT SHADOW

How deeply one you are with our Father, Lord.
How tenderly you share with us all you hear from Him
In the silence of eternity.
One you are with the Pneuma who forms gently
Our lives in the light of Father's words; the Spirit
Who reveals the splendid purpose of divine formation
Of universe and the emergent human race; who
manifests
Your healing touch on our planet and its cruel history.
He shapes our life into the open form of a flower
Reaching for the sun, a chalice waiting to be filled
with light.
He graces our heart with a soft tolerance of the Infinite
That it may not wither under the rays of God's
immensity.
Then He makes us enter into the mystery of divine
formation:
The eternal Event that is the Trinity, awakening us
To your image in our life, that radiant shadow
In our heart of the fullness of the living God.

CHAPTER ELEVEN

THE AGONY OF HIS WITHHOLDING

"In a short time you will no longer see me, and then
a short time later you will see me again."

(Jn. 16:16)

Your words, my Lord, are not meant for your
apostles alone. They carry a message for each human
heart. They speak about your passion, death and
resurrection. The mystical meaning of these events
must form the lives of all who follow you.

"Seeing" cannot be for us a seeing with bodily
eyes as it was for your apostles. Only the eyes of faith
and love can discern your hidden presence, a vision of
grace that goes deeper than that of the images our
bodily eyes behold.

Your image in my soul pervades my fleeting life.
It bursts wide open the arrogant image my ego
presents to me as I journey through this small domain
of time and space. Make me see, cure my blindness.
Grant me the grace to expose myself to the radiation
of your presence. Put my ego in its place. Turn the
arrogant me into the gentle servant of the forming
mystery in the depths of my being. Transform me,

Lord Jesus, into your likeness. Compel me to retire inwardly to look at you with eyes of faith and love. Let me experience that you dwell there as in a holy temple.

You tell me that sometimes you will show yourself to me, at other times you will be hiding. At such moments of withholding I will no longer see you, no matter how well I recollect myself. This teaches me that seeing you is your gift only, not my achievement. It is your way of detaching me from felt consolation so that I may seek you alone. Keep alive in me that calming trust in you, inmost form of my life. Keep permeating my soul with love in spite of your sometimes deafening silence.

With sorrow I admit the many times I cannot see because I am too dispersed in my own concerns. Losing touch with you, I become estranged from the guiding image of my life. My parched soul is tempted to reach out anxiously for images the world offers to fill my emptiness. My life loses the horizon of mystery. It is as if you say to me:

> Persevere in trust if I withhold myself. I promise you, you will see me again a short time later. While you are crying out for me, I dwell within you, secretly firing the desire of your heart. Only a heart formed in longing can be filled with my love. My absence is a school of divine desire. While suffering my withholding the times seems long to you. When your softened heart finds me again, you will see me in a new and richer way. Then the time of grief will seem short and passing.
>
> Even if it was you who left me behind, don't be discouraged or afraid. I am waiting for the sheep that lost their way. Rejoining me, you may suffer for a while the aftermath of your withholding. Lingering shadows of selfishness will for a short time hide me

from your eyes. You will grope in the dark for a presence that keeps eluding you. Persevere in spite of the darkness of a new beginning and you will see me again appearing on the horizon of your life. Learn to live the outward life without losing inwardness, for you would lose the very form of your being.

"I tell you most solemnly, you will be weeping and wailing while the world will rejoice; you will be sorrowful, but your sorrow will turn to joy."

(Jn. 16:20)

Lord, you alone are the heart of history. The world wants to fashion earth and humanity in its own likeness. Utopias abound. They fascinate the crowd for a moment only to disappear without a trace of light. You alone can give harmonious meaning to humanity and its dreams, to cultures and generations, to nature, art, technique, to science and to the ongoing formation of the earth.

Worldly fashioning by itself alone results in a passing proliferation of fads, in an explosion of counterfeit forms applauded today and gone tomorrow. They tear us apart. They set us against one another and delay the coming of the world of the Spirit you promised us.

How could we not weep when you seem expelled from history? Without you it degenerates into a tale without substance and consistency. But the earthly dreamers of utopian schemes delight in your absence. You were an interference in their projects. Our faith in you as the divine form of this world they chided as debilitating, an insult to pride and self-sufficiency. We are called to form this world in your likeness. Our formative presence should be pervaded by your presence. When you become less visible in our formation of earth and history, the world feels relief: *"the world will rejoice; you will be sorrowful."* We are filled with sorrow, they with boundless optimism. They hope finally to realize their dreams in a universe unencumbered by your presence.

In such periods of seeming defeat we need your assurance: *"your sorrow will turn to joy."*

> "A woman in childbirth suffers, because her time has come; but when she has given birth to the child she forgets the suffering in her joy that a man has been born into the world."   *(Jn.* 16:21)

What a striking image of the way a Christian gives form to self and world. Your divine form rests in my soul as a powerful seed straining to be released. Like a child slowly takes form in his mother's womb, so your divine form begins to articulate itself first in all dimensions of my inner life. A mother with child may look to some people less attractive outwardly. She has to slow down and must finally give up for a while her work outside the home. Similarly during periods of inner transformation we feel often less able to bring a Christ-like attractive presence to that part of the vineyard in which we are placed by you. Grace turns our energies inward like the body energies of a woman in whose womb new life begins to emerge.

The more we allow your divine form to articulate itself in our life, the more we may suffer. For our life is already contaminated by the counterfeit forms of this world. They fiercely resist transformation. Gradually you transform us inwardly until our time comes, as it comes for the expecting woman. The time comes when we must allow your divine form to push decisively through the last stubborn forms of life that cover up our divine destiny. This is the time of our rebirth in the form of Jesus — the time of utmost grace and utmost resistance, of cutting the last cord that ties us to our arrogant ego. How much we feel like a woman in childbirth, whose time has come.

"but when she has given birth to the child she forgets the suffering in her joy that a man has been born into the world."

Once I have allowed your divine form to take over my life, a new Christ-like person has been born into the world. Baptismal grace has matured in me sufficiently. The Spirit invites me to move into the world with the transforming power of Jesus. At moments He may make me feel that Jesus' life form shines forth in my daily doings. My joy is then so great that I forget about the sufferings of my inner formation. I no longer remember the pain of the final break through of Jesus' full grown form into my daily life, the cutting of the cord.

Therefore Jesus says:

"So it is with you: you are sad now, but I shall see you again, and your hearts will be full of joy, and that joy no one shall take from you."   *(Jn.* 16:22)

THE AGONY OF YOUR WITHHOLDING

While life flows to its dying time
You form me gently for eternity.
Your presence penetrates me lovingly
With soft illumination.
Sometimes you make me see
The mystery of divine formation
Achieved in history and in me, inwardly.
Then you withdraw again, leaving me
In the agony of your withholding.
Life loses vibrancy,
The hold of time strangles me,
Fills me with anxiety
That muffles thought and action.
The piercing pain of loss
Of the beloved One
Excavates this mourning heart
Until it is deep enough
For cruel longing.
You appear again on the horizon of my vision:
Eternity bursting through the veils of time
Renewing my vigor and my youth.
Gone is the anguish of an empty heart.
Life springs forth as a throbbing child
Straining from the darkness of the womb
Into the fullness of history
To sing the glory of the Lord,
To help transform humanity
Into the likeness of divinity.

CHAPTER TWELVE

THE DAY OF JOY

When that day comes,
you will not ask me any questions.
I tell you most solemnly,
anything you ask for from the Father
he will grant in my name.
Until now you have not asked for anything
      in my name.
Ask and you will receive,
and so your joy will be complete.

(Jn. 16:23-25)

You tell us, Lord, how the power of your presence transforms our soul in the sight of the Father. The Father loves your face in us. Original sin no longer obscures the likeness in which we are created. You implore us to be faithful to the inner formation you granted us.

Faithfulness to your transforming presence means, first of all, that we try not to obscure your image again by personal sin and, if we do so, that we unveil it by confession and repentance.

Faithfulness means that we live and move in the abiding joy of your presence, joy no one can take from us except ourselves.

Faithfulness to your image means that we allow your transforming power to flow out in all dimensions of our life. If we live in fidelity to the mystery of transformation, your life becomes our life, your name our name. We begin to breathe, move, live, and pray in your name alone.

When we ask the Father for the gift of formation of our life, it is no longer us asking. It is you in us. How could the Father refuse us if we ask humbly in your name?

We could never renew life and world by our own force alone. You made known to us that powers of divine formation flow continuously from the Formation Event that is the most blessed Trinity. They fill the universe and our daily situation. They enter our heart more deeply when they are asked for in surrender and adoration.

You make us aware that the life of divine formation is a life of asking the Father, a life of openness to his light and love. Even the asking is not ours. It is the asking of you in us. Help us to abandon ourselves inwardly to your prayerful openness to the Father of all formation.

When we allow you to take us up in your openness, we receive gift after gift. Our heart becomes a treasure house. The treasures spill over into our life. You begin to transform not only our heart but all dimensions of our person and the world we touch by our presence. The joy over your abiding in our inmost being is completed by the joy we feel over your expanding presence in all of our life: *ask and you will receive, and your joy will be complete.* Our trust in your renewing presence becomes so deep that we don't ask you any questions. We abandon ourselves

to you and through you to the Father in openness
and joy: *When that day comes, you will not ask me
any questions.*

> When that day comes
> you will ask in my name;
> and I do not say that I shall pray to the Father for you,
> because the Father himself loves you
> for loving me
> and believing that I came from God.
> I came from the Father and have come into the world
> and now I leave the world to go to the Father.
>
> *(Jn.* 16:26-28)

Often we call your words at the last supper "words
of farewell" and that they are. Yet they are more. They
carry a power and meaning far beyond the final words
of a parent or friend taken away from us never to
return. Your farewell is an end and at the same time a
beginning: the end of one way of dwelling among us,
the beginning of another way of abiding within us.

After your death and resurrection you "pitched
your tent" lastingly among humanity. This event
initiates an unexpected dynamic in human history.
Therefore you tell us here that at the same time
something beautiful has ended and something more
beautiful has begun. You make known to us that you
will insert yourself as a whole new principle of
aliveness in human history, that you will dwell in the
heart of anyone who welcomes you, who can find
words to thank you for this gift of yourself, for this
promise of life abundant and everlasting.

Your announcement of lasting sojourn is at the
same time an invitation. You ask us to enter without
fear into your own relationship with the Father, to
share in your formation by Him in time and eternity.

You make us surrender to the direction which the Holy Spirit gives to your own perennial permeation of cultures and ages. You make clear to us that what happened to you will in some way happen to us. Your formation by the Father and the Spirit will continue in our formation. The unfolding of our life will be a sharing in your unfolding.

If our existence begins to take form in your image, it will be marked by the sublime transitions you describe here: *I came from the Father and have come into the world and now I leave the world to go to the Father.*

With these words you welcome us into the mystery of your own formation. You refer not only to its unfolding on earth but above all to its origin in the ageless divinity. You want to make clear to us that the formation of your life on earth was from the first moment to the last a manifestation of the Father's formative love for us. You want to impress on our hearts that your human unfolding finds its origin and meaning in God alone.

I came from the Father . . . Your human life, Lord Jesus, can be appraised only in the light of this truth. Your Spirit directs us gently through these inspired words to dwell on the Formation Event in the Trinity. Each formative event in your earthly life should be perceived against the horizon of this Eternal Event. Outside this vision of faith we cannot fathom the formative mysteries of your life. They will not touch and transform our hearts in the way they were meant to. Therefore you repeat this truth over and over again in the Gospels *(Jn.* 1:18; 14:6; 3:31) Here also: *the Father himself loves you for loving me and believing that I came from God.*

Divine formation from Eternity makes you the only Mediator of the graced transformation of humanity and world. Because you came from God, you alone can witness what the true formation of life should be. *(Jn.* 1:18) Because you share in the eternal formation you alone can be our way into that mystery. *(Jn.* 14:16) "Who is from the earth belongs to the earth and speaks the language of the earth. Who comes from heaven stands above all." *(Jn.* 3:31)

You come to us, Lord Jesus, not to return alone into the silent splendor of the Formation Event that is the Trinity. You take us with you. You came to share with us a divine form of life, to transform our soul so that we might be able to know in faith our Father as you know Him and to know you as the Father knows you. You came to the world to capture all those who have been given to you by the Father, to bring them home in the eternal mystery of the Divine.

We are invited to share in the formation of you, the Son. Sharing in your formation we come in and with you to the Father. It is true, we did not come from the Father in the same way you did: we are not formed from eternity by the Father. Our own initial formation — unlike yours — has a definite beginning in time and space. But when we live in the faith that you came from the Father you make us share in the eternal formation that is yours. You add to our form of life what is missing because we ourselves did not come forth from the Father in the same way as you. Thus we pray:

THE DAY OF LIGHT

Your day has come, the day of light,
A day of springtime and of flight
From painful isolation.
A day of joy: our inmost face
Lights up in love, with features of your countenance,
The Father falls in love with us.
O, let us never veil again the brightness of your face
In our lonely soul. Let us live in faithfulness
To our Father's voice which calls forth to transparency
The silent form slumbering in our inmost being.
Faithful image of Divinity, awake in us,
Flow out in our life.
Mystery that moves us, every day,
That keeps us in its orbit, not wanting us
To drift away from the sweet captivity of grace.
Your Form at the center of our life
Attracts powers of divine formation
Flowing softly from the Trinity, filling
Universe and history with gentle persuasion.
You make our heart a treasure house;
By simply touching it, it gains a new vibration,
Waves of grace and love undulate
In the lagoon of our stilted life
Spilling over in the regions of abandonment
Surrounding our shores.
You pitched your tent in our soul.
You leave us free to lift its curtain
Allowing you to make your way.
Should we keep it closed
You may never see the light of day;
Kept away from love and adoration
You are not allowed to shine forth
In the daily situation
Crying out for the touch of the divine.

Let us share the bread and wine
Of Father's table in the sanctuary of our soul.
Let the unfolding of our life
Share your unfolding in our interiority.
Hide us in the splendor of the Trinity
To venture out as gentle knights of Light,
As symphonies of the Spirit
In a universe of dissonance.

CHAPTER THIRTEEN

HUMAN WORDS AND FAITH FORMATION

"I have been telling you all this in metaphors, the hour is coming when I shall no longer speak to you in metaphors; but tell you about the Father in plain words." *(Jn.* 16:25)

Your disciples, Lord, like we ourselves do not always understand what you try to communicate to prosaic human minds. We are not only small-minded but also literal-minded. Too often we are satisfied with the surface meaning of your words and don't dive deeper into their message. They become signs of information not carriers of a transcendent beauty that transforms our lives. Their silent wisdom eludes our grasping intellect.

The hour you are speaking about is the hour of the Holy Spirit. It is the hour of our formation in you between your first and second coming. The hour in which the Holy Spirit prepares our spirit to hear and heed your human words. The hour in which he fills our hearts with longing for your presence.

You promise us that in the hour that is coming you will tell us about the Father not in metaphors but in words that are plain. This does not mean that your words will be changed into new ones that would be instantly clear and transparent. Your words are meant to form our faith. Faith is a gift of light and darkness. Faith is about divine mysteries that cannot be penetrated by human cleverness. Faith does not open up to the splendor of lucidity but to that of mystery.

Words of faith formation point to your mystery without exhausting its riches. The words that form faith work by comparison, symbol and reference. Unveiling they veil, unconcealing they conceal. The gift of faith is your gift alone; it attunes to realities that infinitely transcend human experience.

To express what is beyond expression we need symbols and metaphors. You had to use comparisons with daily events to grant us a glimpse of divine truths that should form mind and heart, life and action. When you reveal to us the Truth of the Father and of the Formation Event that gives form to your sonship, you use words that usually describe relationships within the human family. There are no other words than human words to foster faith formation; they serve well as long as we know that they do not, cannot exhaust the mystery.

You yourself gave us the example in the faith formation of your disciples. They took your words in a literal sense. They missed their gentle pointing to profounder realities. How often you had to correct their misconceptions. You even had to do it again at the end of your life.

How touching is your patience, Jesus. How gently you took the defeat of your attempt to make them approach mystery in silent acceptance. How impatient we are by comparison. We want our projects to come true instantly. We are irritated, even desperate, if people do not grasp what we communicate. We are inclined to impose on them what they are not ready for, to use force instead of persuasion. Grant us the gift of waiting for what cannot be accomplished willfully. Let compassion replace imposition. Let us flow patiently with people and situations. Be our patience, Lord Jesus.

What you announce for the hour that is coming is not an exhausting analysis of divine realities, an emptying of the secret of the Infinite. The mystery will remain mystery. What you promise is the infusion of an enlightened sensitivity for the deeper meaning of your words. The Holy Spirit will refine the human spirit, attuning it to the formative power of Revelation. Even then, to foster formation in faith, we must enter into the Truth of the divine through the portals of human words sanctified by you. They are like angels with flaming swords that guard the paradise of faith. Those who try to pass them by will be slain. The garden of revelation should not be entered lightly; neither can it be conquered by human wisdom. Only those are allowed within its borders who are guided by the Spirit. They grow in ever deeper understanding. They may touch the mystery your words are pointing to.

This is the story of ongoing faith formation. A faith that is much more than mere intellectual assent. A faith that is obscure yet knows pockets of light between long spans of darkness. You make us grow from faith form to faith form in a journey of graced transcendence. Each new form becomes a dynamic, formative power in our Christian life. You invite us again and again to return, in meditative dwelling, to the everlasting words that once initiated Christian faith formation. You ask us to dwell patiently until the Holy Spirit discloses richer meanings at your bidding.

How naive your disciples were when they thought that now they understood all you meant to say: "Now you are speaking plainly and not using metaphors." *(Jn.* 16:29-30)

You reproach them mildly with words that are partly a question:

"Do you believe at last? Listen, the time will come in fact it has come already — when you will be scattered each going his own way and leaving me alone and yet I am not alone, because the Father is with me."

(Jn. 16:31-32)

They imagine the hour of explanation has come, the time of clarification of any obscurity, the scaling down of mystery to our small, created mind. Vainly you try to tell your friends that it is rather the moment of faith they are invited to. You tell them how feeble their faith still is, for it is not yet immersed in the hidden ground of your words and metaphors. Feeble faith will not prevent unfaithfulness of life. Indeed they soon will leave you alone.

You are still speaking directly to your disciples. After this, in the remainder of the discourse, you will no longer speak to us or them. You will speak lovingly not to us but about us in a wonderful prayer to the Father. Before this prayer, you close your farewell with a last encouragement:

"I have told you all this that you may find peace in me. In the world you will have trouble but be brave: I have conquered the world."

(Jn. 16:33)

You just told them that they would leave you alone. You tried to soften the impact that their own betrayal might have on them when they would come to the painful realization that your prediction has come true. You do not want them to feel that their unfaithfulness means a break between you and them. You want to prevent that they remember your prediction as a reproach that keeps eating away at their heart for a lifetime. They should remember your word not in pain but in faith. That you had foreseen all of this should strengthen their faith in you. It corresponds with similar sayings in this discourse. "I have told you all this, so that when the time for it comes you remember that I told you." *(Jn.* 16:4) "I have told you this now before it happens, so when it does happen you may believe that I am He." *(Jn.* 13:19)

Lord Jesus, your concern is a consolation for us who are feeble in faith as your disciples were. You warn us of our frailty of heart and spirit. We don't take that warning seriously until we realize that we have left you alone again. At that moment of awareness we are overcome by guilt and shame. Red-faced we hesitate to return to you. But you keep telling us to find peace in you. What you ask of us in the moment of remorse is a deepening of faith in your love and forgiveness. Even betrayal can become a step to intimacy if we surrender more fully to your mercy.

In this final word of farewell, the assurance of your peace carries also a wider meaning than that of consolation in the midst of suffering and failure. "In the world you will have trouble, but be brave: I have conquered the world." *(Jn.* 16:33)

Like you, Lord Jesus, we will always lose in this world. In the mysterious battle between the divine and the demonic, darkness seems to win out so often.

Oppression, ridicule, subtle or open persecution will be the fate of Christians in this age. You seem to be the loser and yet you are the victor. In the end you will be revealed as the divine conqueror of the world.

You want our faith in your victory to be the source of our peace. This peace is not merely an equanimity of heart in the midst of rejection by the world. It is far more. In faith we enjoy already your everlasting victory in which we share.

Here on earth your triumph is hidden under the humiliations of your Church and your saints. It is the vision of faith that makes life a daily celebration of your victory. The deeper our faith formation, the more your final triumph becomes the luminous horizon of our days. Our demeanor begins to radiate the lighthearted certainty of the Eschaton. Disappointments about darkness within and without your pilgrim Church no longer draw us down.

The peace you grant us in this vision is stronger than an inner mood. It is a conviction of victory rooted in faith formation that is nourished by a dwelling on your everlasting words. "Heaven and earth will pass away, but my words will not pass away." *(Mark* 13:31) Indeed, without vision people will perish. How powerful is the vision announced in the book of Revelation: "It is he who is coming on the clouds; everyone will see him, even those who pierced him, and all the races of the earth will mourn over him. This is the truth. Amen. 'I am the Alpha and the Omega' says the Lord God, who is, who was, and who is to come, the Almighty'."

"Those who prove victorious will be dressed, like these, in white robes; I shall not blot their names out of the book of life, but acknowledge their names in the presence of my Father and his angels." *(Rev.* 3:5,6)

St. Paul witnesses for that joy that emerges from our faith formation: "With God on our side who can be against us? . . . Nothing therefore can come between us and the love of Christ, even if we are troubled or worried, or being persecuted, or lacking food or clothes, or being threatened or even attacked. As scripture promised: for your sake we are being massacred daily and reckoned as sheep for the slaughter. These are the trials through which we triumph, by the power of him who loved us. For I am certain of this: neither death nor life, no angel, no prince, nothing that exists, nothing still to come, not any power, or height or depth, nor any created thing, can ever come between us and the love of God made visible in Christ Jesus our Lord."

SPRINGS OF SILENT BEAUTY

Your words are springs of silent beauty.
They purify the sordid mind,
They wind their way through the decay
Of listless thoughts that sink and fall
Like withered autumn leaves on heavy hearts.
Your words are like a melody that fills the soul
With gentle sound and then abounds in all of life.
Your words are filled with mystery,
Unveiling, they still veil the Holy Grail.
Expressing what is beyond expression
They grant a fleeting glimpse
Of what transcends the greedy mind.
Your words teach us to wait
For what shall not be attained willfully
In the wasteland of blind self-exertion.
Your words make us flow compassionately
With all you allow to be in our limping lives.
Refine the coarseness of the human heart,
Defy its arrogance, attune it to those sacred words,
Those holy portals to the mysteries of faith,
Those angels with the flaming swords
That guard the paradise of Revelation.
We shall be slain when we scale down your mystery
To restless minds, arrogant and small.
We shall be scattered outside your garden
In the deserts of a dismal world.
For feeble faith cannot prevent unfaithfulness of life.
When we are being massacred daily for your name,
Restore a living faith in your victory which we share
While being stepped upon and slandered everywhere.
Let Eschaton shine forth in us
While being slaughtered by the infamous,
For precious in your eyes are the deaths
Of faithful ones. Their names are written large
In the lasting book of life.

CHAPTER FOURTEEN

THE PRIESTLY PRAYER

St. John: Chapter Seventeen

The seventeenth chapter of St. John's Gospel has been honored with a beautiful name. It is called: the priestly prayer of Jesus. The chapter could be read meditatively as a complement to a reading of the thirteenth chapter of the first letter of St. Paul to the Corinthians. That chapter is called by tradition "the hymn to love." In it St. Paul exalts the love of Christ as the main forming power of life.

These titles highlight the meaning of the texts for our formation. St. Paul's hymn to love forms our transcendent aspiration for divine love. This ability for divine love is the gift of the Spirit to our soul. When baptism transfigured our soul into the image of Christ, this potency for divine love was infused in us. This dynamic principle is not meant to remain hidden in our soul. It must be released into our concrete experiential life, transforming it into the living likeness of Christ. The sublime fruit of that transformation is our daily sacrifice of life in service of God and fellow human beings. Jesus' priestly prayer is about that sacrifice.

Christian love is released from the soul to foster first of all the inner formation of the Christian. Without that conversion we could not be a formative presence to others. As long as we are inwardly deformed by lack of love for ourselves in God, we are unable to love others. Christians who cannot appraise and accept the gifts and limits God allows in their lives cannot appreciate similar gifts and limits in those they live with day by day. When the pride form prevails in life, it obscures the radiance of the love of Jesus. He alone can conquer human pride and its devastations. He alone can cure the anxieties, insecurities and self-condemnations pride gives rise to.

Concomitantly, with this inner formation, we begin to experience a transformation of our attitudes toward others. Jesus' love begins to break through in our daily encounters with people. We become less manipulative and demanding. We are more willing to forgive and forget, more ready to make ourselves available within the limits of our life call and possibility.

Formation that happens between people could be called interformation. Interformation in Christ implies an incarnation into our human relationships of the love of our Lord. His love begins to permeate both our inner life and our interactions with others once we allow it to issue forth from our soul. It reaches its height when it inspires a total oblation of self to God. At that moment the love of Christ shines forth in a priestly way.

What are the marks of the priestly love of Jesus? Jesus offers his whole life for others. He lays it down so that they too may be formed in the love of the Father. His sacrifice is a prayer that people may escape the power of the pride principle in their soul.

He begs the Father to help them elude the deformative world of self-exaltation that surrounds them and
tempts them to crave for glory, power and possession.
He asks his Father to defeat the divisive influence of
the evil one always playing on the excessive need for
vainglory in fallen humanity.

He wants us to share in his priestly gift of life and
in the spirit that animates his giving. The sacrifice of
self with Jesus is unlike the sacrifices made by us as
worldly people. It is not to gain advance and advantage for ourselves or to gain recognition. Our sacrifice
like his is only for the glory of the Father. It must be
in tune, as Jesus prays, with Father's word, with what
he wants us to do, not only inwardly but also
outwardly in the world he entrusts to our daily
formation. What he wants us to do is gradually
disclosed to us by the Holy Spirit. The Spirit uses for
this communication the various formation phases of
life and the succession of life situations. This sacrifice
is not only the gift of our life at the end of our sojourn
but an oblation daily renewed; it is the daily priestly
surrender of self to the role we are called to play in the
mystery of formation that slowly forms humanity,
world and history.

Participation in the mystery of the interformation of humanity demands from us the sacrifice of our
innate search for private glory. We have to die to that
principle of division that poisons humanity. Our
sharing together with others in the divine formation
of the world demands the same kind of giving. We
cannot truly serve God's direction for this world as
long as we are fascinated by projects that contradict
his designs.

That our function in the divine formation of
world and humanity cannot be clear at once is

another source of sacrificial living. No sooner have we settled down in one way of living than a new situation, an inner or outer change, a phase of maturation reveals that this is not yet wholly the way meant for us. This disclosure by the Spirit is unsettling. We are called to share again in the priestly sacrifice of Jesus. We may have to give up for the glory of the Father cherished customs and dispositions, familiar surroundings, perhaps even popularity with family, friends and colleagues. As we change, we may offend the pride principle in people by our newly formed simplicity. Unwittingly, we may incur their condemnation. Such periods of transition can be real crisis experiences. Such a crisis enables us to disclose a little more the mysterious life form in Jesus the Father calls us to. The transcendence crisis is also an occasion to restore and deepen our participation in Jesus' priestly sacrifice of life. It reminds us that our life is far from perfect, that it is only on the road towards likeness with the sacrificial life of Jesus.

Above all what marks our participation in the daily oblation of Jesus' life is the spirit of prayer. The unfolding sacrifice of our life in service of the divine direction of history and humanity can only please the Father if it is permeated by prayerful presence. Jesus, turning to the Father in priestly prayer at the end of his life is meant to form us in that presence.

The priestly prayer of Jesus is not one of gloom and sadness. On the contrary it is filled with adoration and the joy of thanksgiving. Before he leaves the intimacy and protection of the last meal with his friends, he lifts his heart in prayer to the Father.

What is to come is dreadfully near now. The setting may seem desperate to us, but it does not deter Jesus. Before this moment of divine intimacy between

Father and Son, Jesus had spoken to his friends. Now He speaks to his Father alone. Only once after this prayer will he speak somewhat extensively to others before his death. After that he finds shelter in divine silence, an inner continuation of prayer to the Father interrupted only by a few brief words: responses to his judges, short exhortations to his disciples, invocations of the Father. He is still bodily among people but his heart already transcends in prayer the frontiers of humanity. He celebrates the Formation Event of the Trinity where he alone is infinitely at home. He expresses this prayer of divine transcendence in words so that we may be formed by them over the centuries to come. For we are called to share by grace in the same Formation Event that makes him the Eternal Son of God. All that is to happen to Jesus is taken up in advance within this prayer. He expresses his love in powerful words of thanksgiving and adoration. Shortly hereafter he will express the same with his blood. While his captors will deprive him of all external dignity, his prayer now radiates the sublime dignity of his love and freely given self surrender.

His prayer sounds festive as the proclamation of Eucharist. At times this prayer reaches the height of exultation. The words *glorify, glorified, glory* emerge again and again. They set the tone and provide the recurrent theme of joy that marks this last song of Jesus' heart on earth.

The Lord pours his whole being into these words of adoration and thanksgiving. He thanks the Father for allowing him to sacrifice his life for the formation of a new creation that will share in the Eternal Formation Event of God. He also consecrates us in this prayer to a participation in his divine life and sacrifice.

PRIESTLY PRAYER

Priestly prayer of the Lord,
Joyful word of adoration,
Saying thanks in an oblation
Of human life.
Song of love, of aspiration,
Consecrating everything
We say and do.

Priestly prayer
Rising softly
From your likeness in the soul
Released into our longing heart,
Pervading life with sacrifice
And sweet surrender.

Priestly prayer
Healing the self despisal
That unexpected failure
Breeds in excited minds,
Winding down
Into the chambers of anxiety
That imprison potencies for joy.

Priestly prayer
Slaying foolish pride,
Poison of humanity, source of war,
Mother of cruelty and subtle slander,
Blight on the community of humankind.

O let your priestly prayer
Lift degraded life
To a festive prayer of Eucharist
In the midst of persecution
By the Evil One.

CHAPTER FIFTEEN

DREAD OF THE
DIVINE AND MOST ABANDONED SOULS

After saying this, Jesus raised his eyes to heaven and said: "Father, the hour has come." (Jn. 17:1)

You address God as "Father," this word of intimacy hidden as a jewel in all your prayers. It does not stay concealed within your communication. Rather it shines forth as a soft and steady light into your nights and days. Its meaning keeps your movements light-hearted, resilient and graceful. You feel loved by him continuously, buoyed up and carried by his presence. You invite us gently to share in your life and its feeling of graced vitality, to become graceful and light-hearted because God is our Father too.

Life wounds and scares us. We feel lonely in crowds that seem to carry us along like leaves floating aimlessly in a hurried stream. You gently gather up the leaves that are lost. You give them life, your life, life with the Father. To share your life is to share your convictions. The deepest conviction that refreshed and sustained you was always one and the same: God is Father. He loves me. He does what is best for me. He does not interfere with the free will of those who mistreat me. He helps me to cope with evil and misunderstanding, to make the best of it.

God is like a kind human father who helps his child to sustain the loss and adversity he cannot prevent from happening to him. He surrounds us all with the best of care. He bends over our daily lives in love and affirmation.

Do I, as his child, really share your conviction of the Father's love? Do I share it when the hour of failure and disappointment suddenly strikes? When depression creeps treacherously into my heart? Is God a Father for me? The exquisite One who brightens my days and frees my heart? Or do I secretly fear God? Is he for me a merciless master? A resentful overseer? A taskmaster ready to pounce on every mistake?

You came to free us from irritational guilt and fear, from the dreadful perfectionism that comes in their wake. How prone we are to be fearful of God. The awe of his majesty, his dazzling purity, his mighty justice fill us with suspicion. You know better than we how dread of the Divine disturbed humanity over the ages. Religions of dread emerged from this anxiety. In some of them people were sacrificed to placate your Father, whom they did not know. They tore out human hearts, sacrificing them wantonly to temper the divine wrath. They imagined God's anger as a deadly cloud, as a somber sky hanging over humanity oppressively, ready to inflict punishment and destruction without measure.

You came to heal that festering wound. You taught people to pray to God as their Father. Did your message reach me, Jesus? Did it touch my heart, still my fear, calm the guilt that eats away at me? Or are there still shadows in my life of a primitive dread of the Divine? This deadly cancer poisons human life.

It is the cancer at the heart of false religion and fictitious spirituality. Is your prayer to the Father setting me free every day a little more? Or does the old dread deform your teaching of love? Does your teaching become one burden more to weigh me down?

We meet people who have left your teachings. They say with conviction: leaving them was a relief. They never experienced God as Father. They misinterpreted your message. Perhaps their parents were paralyzed by the old anxiety. God was only a judge for them, not a Father who understands and forgives, who gently affirms all hesitant attempts to grow and unfold. They formed their children in their own anxious image. The father in their family became the image not of a God of love but of a God of wrath.

They suffered the worst form of child abuse: not abuse of the body but abuse of the mind. Their vulnerable mind was poisoned. A false image of fatherhood began to form their life. They heard you speak about God as Father. It did not evoke in them the image of a God of love. Your word reminded them of their own forbidding father, of others who played a domineering father-role in their lives. It spoiled your word for them. The hold of dread of the divine resumed its power, so in panic they fled away from you.

Let all of us share, O Lord, in your awareness of the Father's love. Cure the dread of the Divine that hardens hearts and poisons minds. Heal the wounds of childhood that left so many souls — in the midst of material abundance — spiritually abandoned and alone. Especially touch the most poor and abandoned souls among them. Their inner poverty and misery is camouflaged by a well-nourished body, an educated mind, by suburban homes and glittering cars.

How much more abandoned they are than simple people here and abroad who believe in divine powers no matter how little understood. How difficult it is to reach these most abandoned souls. How little they reward those who come in your name. They withhold the gratitude and admiration simple people bestow so generously. How we fear their pride and arrogance, their sarcasm and skepticism, their learning and sophistication. How much we prefer the awe and sympathy others less educated may bestow. So often they satisfy our need to feel needed.

Leaving these recalcitrant, most abandoned souls to their own sophistication, we may travel far away to find less abandoned persons who will comply more easily with our words and grant us the worship we may unwittingly desire. It is good and necessary to be an image of your Father for less abandoned and simple people, but let this motivation not become a pretext to prevent others from caring for those who are most abandoned of soul because of their physical well being and sophistication. Don't allow us to forget them in spite of the pain their cynicism may cause. Also, for these most poor you gave your blood, not only for the simple and pleasant people who make us feel so needed, generous and good. Give us the grace to keep trying to melt the wall of refusal that imprisons their wounded hearts.

DREAD OF THE DIVINE

Dread of the Divine
That turns the heart
Into a mine
Of black despair.
How can we bear
With the wrath
That haunts our path
Like a vulture
Poised to pounce
On the race
That culture after culture
Wards off the raid
Off irate gods.
Dread of the Divine
Born in souls worn out
By abandonment and guilt.
The anger of the gods
Became the deadly cloud,
The somber sky
Hanging down oppressively
Over humanity in fear,
Threatening to rain
Hailstones of affliction.
Dread of the Divine,
Cancer that poisons
Human life,
Source of strife,
Burden that weighs down
Our flight to the stars.
. . . You came
As the defenseless babe
Of Bethlehem.

The lighthearted boy
Of Nazareth,
The gentle friend
Of abandoned souls
In Israel,
The sufferer
On a cross
To restore our loss
Of trust in God
As Father
Who does not hover
As a vulture over
Our dissolving life,
Who wants our peace,
Not affliction, strife,
Who gathers us tenderly
As fallen leaves
From a dying tree
Miraculously
Restored to life.

CHAPTER SIXTEEN

THE CLOSURE OF THE EARTHLY WINDOW

Father, the hour has come:
glorify your Son
so that your Son may glorify you.

(Jn. 17:1)

Father, the hour has come. Before this last
supper, Lord, you had often said to your disciples:
"My hour has not yet come." You meant the summit
of your mission was not yet to be celebrated. That was
to be reserved for the hour of the consummation of
your gentle life. But now the hour has come. Your
attunement to the Father makes you sense that *this is
it.* You affirm the hour, you say "yes" to it. You do
not make much to-do about it. You accept that it is
here and flow silently with its mysterious momentum.
The only thing that counts for you is conformity to
your Father's will. You call it simply 'the hour.'

For us too there will be that special hour: the
finale of our life. An hour we cannot escape, the hour
of the closure of our earthly window.

How we live that hour of sorrow and faith will
give final form to our existence. All that went before
will be of no avail if we do not know how to surrender

to this mysterious moment of life's transition. To be sure, our body will rebel as yours did in the garden. Deepen our faith, Lord Jesus, that in the end you will enable us to surrender like you to the Father's desire in trust and love. Grant us your attunement to the Father that we too may sense that it is not cruel fate but Eternal Love that sets this final stage for our life.

Your whole passage on earth was a reaching out towards this moment of dramatic closure. It loomed steadily before you, it was threatening and beckoning at the same time. It was very much present in its absence. Therefore, you said so often: "The hour has not yet come."

Grant us the wisdom to live in the light of that hour which steadily approaches. Make our days like gentle waves in fluent harmony with the shores that are awaiting us. Every day many are summoned to face that night. Assist them, Jesus, in their agony. Touch them with the sweetness of your surrender to the Eternal. Make their final hour the finest, no matter what went before. Your compassion heals wounds, softens pain, relieves fears, forgives sins, if we only flow with it in gentle surrender.

To be mindful of the hour makes us less inclined to abandon our souls in pursuit of pleasure and glory. A life-long hunt for human esteem will make it difficult to seek and find the divine glory at the decisive moment of our pilgrimage. The pride form that permeates our fallen life leads to the abandonment of your image and form in the inmost depths of our being. The more we allow pride to proliferate in our life, the more it will weigh us down at the moment we receive the Father's invitation to share in your ascent to the Divine.

Preparing for your hour of ascent in agony you pray: "Glorify your Son so that your Son may glorify you." These words highlight the profound meaning of this hour. You put its deepest sense in one word you repeat again and again. That word is "glory." Glory is proper to God. Glory marks God as God. Glory lets God appear as God. It is the manifestation of the splendor of God's being.

Therefore, only God can be glorified as ultimate goodness, truth and beauty. Only he can let his divine glory shine forth in anything created. He does so above all in your sacred humanity. So you pray: "Glorify your Son." You ask your Father that his glory may manifest itself in the hour of defeat and death. This is your way of saying: "I surrender to your will, Father. I do not ask for human glory; only your glory counts for me. I may look like a fool in the eyes of people. They see me as an abysmal failure. They scorn me as a dreamer who lived in vain for a fleeting mirage that could never come true. They scoff at me as a grandiose carpenter of Nazareth who ends his life a criminal between thieves on a cross. Father, I accept the sacrifice of my honor in this world. May your glory alone radiate in my failed life and broken body."

You pray that this divine glorification may come true. You pray for it because you know it goes beyond human powers to bear with the debasement of beauty in mind and body. To be glorified in this hour implies both the wanton destruction by others of anything in your appearance that can evoke esteem in worldly people and your entering into the true splendor of the Divine. Once you put it tersely: "The Messiah must suffer and so enter into his glory." How deeply you knew that obedience and humility open human nature to divine glorification. You already taste the glory in the debasement that is waiting you.

You pray further: "Glorify your Son so that your Son may glorify you." The Father turns your defeat into glory. But you too aspire to manifest the power and splendor of the Father. You do so by showing us how you surrender to the Father in the obedience that carries your passion and death. You praise the Father by your fidelity to the final form he wants your life to take. When all this is over, you will glorify the Father lastingly. When the Father has raised you up, you will not rest only in the gift of your own glorified humanity. You want the Father to be praised by countless others who share in your glorification. By the power of your Spirit you will transform our lives. In us you want to be present as a transforming power in history. You embrace the desperate multitudes who populate the earth as it rotates slowly to its end, a mere speck of dust in the vast cosmos.

Your friend, Therese of Lisieux, tells us that she does not imagine her heaven as a place of enjoyment only. She envisages it as a lasting opportunity to do good to people on earth. This vision is in tune with your Spirit and with the message of your priestly prayer. To be glorified ourselves is not the highest goal we can reach. The highest form of life is to glorify God, to be a living candle of devotion to his name, to make him known everywhere, to help hearts to create room for him.

If you would have prayed only, "Glorify your Son," your prayer could have been understood as narrowness of vision. It might have obscured for us the scope of your mission. But when you add, "so that your Son may glorify you," everything comes into movement with these words; it shall never stop again. In these words you reveal to us that God incarnated the glory of his Divine, Eternal Form in your human form. Your glorified nature becomes the formation principle of our Christian life, the wellspring of our transformation in you, the path through suffering into glory. You have become the focal point in the universe where the loving formation power of God can pour itself out limitlessly into a hapless humanity that has lost touch with the divine form of life in which it was created.

GENTLE CLOSURE

You gently close
The window of this life.
You end its strife,
Bringing our ship
Into your port,
Displacing our worry
With your glory,
Dispelling what is base
By the glory of your face.

Make us repent
The ways we went
Astray, away from home
To build the dome
Of human glory,
To tell the story
Of things achieved
Leaving you alone
To grieve.

Make our days
Like gentle waves
That rise and fall in harmony
With the music of eternity
Until the end of time
When the secret rhyme
Of our lives
Will stand revealed

Embrace, O Lord
The multitudes
That populate this planet
Rotating slowly
To its burial,
Speck of dust
In the vault
Of silent universe.

CHAPTER SEVENTEEN

CONSONANCE WITH
ETERNAL LIFE FORMATION

Through the power over all mankind that you
have given him,
let him give eternal life to all those you
have entrusted to him.

(Jn. 17:2)

While preparing for your passion and death for us, you are already aware of the power of grace and salvation that will be yours because of it. At this moment your heart goes out not only to your Father but to all people. Because of your redeeming death, all humanity will be entrusted to your care. Your heart embraces each person ever to walk the earth. You delight that it will be in your power to give them eternal life.

Your Father formed humanity in the divine image. Each person was called to express that form of God uniquely in his or her life. Since the Fall it has become difficult for us to keep in tune with this foundational form of God in our soul.

How deeply you knew that our daily life was no longer animated by the image of your eternal Father.

Our everyday living was no longer consonant with the eternal life of God imaged in our soul. Our life became empty, pedestrian, and narrow-minded. We had lost the power to keep in touch with the Eternal Source.

You restore this power of consonance with the mystery of eternal life formation. Through the gift of your power, people come in touch again with the divine image in their soul. Your form of life permeates our daily formation, giving it the radiance of eternity. It not only restores us to our divine image, but it elevates us so that we may share in the mystery of divine formation that is the Holy Trinity.

In you, the Son and the Eternal Word, we participate in the eternal formation of that Word in the bosom of the Holy Trinity. Our human minds will never be able to comprehend the infinite generosity of God giving you this power to make us share in the inner eternal formative life of the Godhead.

Help us, Jesus, not to live in forgetfulness of the miracle of love that has happened to us without our deserving it. Grant us the gift of sanctifying memory. Help us to live in the remembrance of the eternal life that wells up in our inmost being because of your mysterious presence there.

> And eternal life is this:
> to know you,
> the only true God,
> And Jesus Christ whom you have sent.

(Jn. 17:3)

You tell us, Jesus, what this sharing in the eternal mystery of divine formation really means. You explain to us that it is a kind of knowing of your Father as the only true God. This special kind of knowledge implies also a knowing of you as being sent, as going forth from God.

What is the kind of knowing you are speaking about? We could call it a formative knowledge, a knowledge that is not simply a question of information, but rather one of formation of our deepest being. It is a formative knowledge about God as he truly and only is, far beyond anything we can conceive or imagine.

It is a knowledge of the heart, a knowledge of love and surrender. A knowledge that lets us wholeheartedly share in the mystery of the divinity.

It is a knowledge of love and longing that only you can grant us. A knowledge which, when grown to fullness, will satiate our restless desire for the abundance of peace and joy. A knowledge which presupposes that we are so grasped by the reality of the divine that our whole existence is permeated and changed by it.

In this sense, Lord Jesus, the growing, living knowledge of God which you grant to us truly transforms our life.

You add to it that eternal life is also a knowing of you, Jesus Christ, who has been sent by the Father. You want to make clear to us that we are called to have a living and transforming knowledge of the God who has made himself known in you, the Son. You try to make us aware again that we are called to share in the eternal formation mystery of the Holy Trinity.

In this mystery your Father knows himself in you, the Son, as the eternal divine image and form of the Father. Also, you, the Son, know yourself in the Father.

Everything has been entrusted to me by my Father;
and no one knows the Son except the Father, just
as no one knows the Father except the Son and those
to whom the Son chooses to reveal him.

(Mt. 11:27)

Before your revelation we did not know anything
about the interformative life of God. Because we
knew nothing about it, we could not live in faith the
mystery of the life of the Holy Trinity and of our
participation in that life. In this prayer you change all
of this. You ask the Father to grant us a share in the
life of God himself. In your prayer you communicate
to us that this life of God is a life of inner communication. Through this interformation it becomes one
life in three persons. The eternal life you give to us is a
sharing in the forming knowledge of these three
divine persons.

This sharing happens in the darkness of faith: it
is a believing knowing and a knowing believing that
gradually transforms the way in which we express
your divine life form in our daily living.

EPIPHANY OF PEACE

Shalom is your legacy,
Peace of mind
For those you left behind
To die in ignomy.
Your broken body
Is an epiphany
Of peace
For suffering humanity.
The sun breaks gloriously
From behind the clouds
Drenching us in light.
So is the might
Of each beam of peace
Piercing our night
Out of a gaping wound
Around each rusty nail.
Peace is the tale
Of redeemed humanity.
Transfigured are
The lakes and mountains,
Fresh, resplendent
Flowers, woods and fountains,
Pristine beauty
Clothes the meadow.
Everything seems soft and mellow,
Everything is new again
Because the Lord is slain.

CHAPTER EIGHTEEN

THE ETERNAL EXIT FROM
THE CAGE OF TIME

And eternal life is this:
to know you,
the only true God,
and Jesus Christ whom you have sent.

(Jn. 17:3)

Your hour has come. Striking is your prayer for us at this crucial moment. Awaiting you is sorrow, suffering, death. Yet it does not occur to you to ask the Father to spare you the torture. You beg him to let you bear the affliction in a surrender that shall glorify his name. Then you ask that your passion may bring eternal life to those entrusted to you.

Your prayer lights up the meaning of this gift. Eternal life is a life of transforming knowledge. Not a mere intellectual understanding but a knowing of the heart that involves our whole being. It is the gift of a living presence to the Divine and to you, Lord Jesus, for you have been sent as the Epiphany of the infinite mystery that embraces creation and penetrates silently its history. Sometimes you spoke about this life of presence as something beautiful that is already ours here and now. At other moments you reveal it as something mysterious ahead of us in the hereafter. It is really both. We are called to this presence already here yet it will be limited until we are liberated for the splendor of the hereafter.

Often we lose the peace of dwelling with the Eternal. It is interrupted by the cares of this age. But the spring for its renewal hides within us. You dwell in our inmost center as a living presence to the Father. This presence is a continuation and unique manifestation of your eternal face to face communion with him. We are called to participate in what you are in the depths of our being. You are in us a source of loving participation in divine reality. Christian life and its formation flows from that participation. In your light we taste divine generosity, patience, humility and formative love. This experience creates a new set of life directives. In the light of your Spirit we appraise them wisely. Once they are rightly appraised and gratefully accepted they inspire and enable us to give form to life in a new fashion. Your presence in us begins to disclose the eternal way. The more you enable us to make it our way, the more our life can be called eternal. For it begins to image in time the divine life lived in eternity. No longer do we drift along anxiously and somewhat confused. No longer is our life restricted to the pursuit of some casual ambitions or the eager fulfillment of few vital needs. No longer is there "no exit" from the cage of time at the end of which our life seems to peter out meaninglessly.

Thanks to your gift daily pursuits receive an eternal significance. Failures and disappointments, suffering and dying are taken up in the eternal meaning you bestow on our lost and forlorn days. The winters of life are the dreary periods of forgetfulness of the eternal spark within. But then you lift us again beyond our protective safety zone into the beyond of the Eternal Spring. Your light penetrates our clouded window. Such moments of awakening form the slender thread of our life direction. No longer ingrained in our petty endeavors, we experience how the formative thread of eternity weaves in and through the pattern of earthly existence. We sense the unfolding movement of the eternal life within us. We experience it as a silent invitation to rise above what we have become.

When we fail to allow the spark of eternity to shine forth in our daily doings, we may be commended for the efficiency of performance, for a job well attended to, but our voyage is no longer an inspiration for fellow travellers. Only when your eternal life carries us do we sail comfortably along the mysterious voyage of life. If we are in touch with the flow of our eternal life, we are able to flow flexibly with the tide of formative events and situations. They are the changing landscapes surrounding our journey and allowed by you in gentle love. Your mystery within us is the lighthouse that guides our frail ships as they toss in the churning waters of history. You want our fragile barks to glide in harmony with the eternal life that is our precious compass. To pamper the pride form of life is to veil the treasure within. You invite us to pull away from the shore of human security and sail out into the ocean of mystery trusting that you will keep afloat the battered bark of our poor lives.

You stress, Lord Jesus, that our eternal life is not only to know the true God, but you yourself whom he has sent. Only through you can we know the mystery of divine life. To know you means to receive the grace of intimacy with you. In that intimacy we experience the revelation of the eternal life of the Trinity. We begin to know God in a new and profound way. For what you call knowing God is not like our many other ways of knowing. You speak about a knowledge of the enlightened heart that fulfills any desire we may have. It is a mystical knowledge in which we are grasped so totally by the truth of God's being that our whole life becomes penetrated by this loving awareness. We should realize that you, as a Semite, use Semitic words to express to us the divine mysteries. The Semitic word for knowing is far less intellectualistic than our Western words for knowledge. It is filled with far more meaning, more profound and comprehensive, more alive and personal, more creative and dynamic. Ultimately you speak here about the loving presence of the Father to you and you to the Father. You tell us that we are called to share in that eternal mystery. We are touched here again by the Trinitarian Formation Event. You rejoice in the Father who has made himself known in you, his eternal Son. You reveal to us that the Father knows himself in the Son and the Son in the Father.

> Everything has been entrusted to me by my Father; and no one knows the Son except the Father, just as no one knows the Father except the Son and those to whom the Son chooses to reveal him.
>
> *(Mt.* 11:27)

As long as we don't know God in his interformative life, we are unable to participate inwardly in this mystery of Divine Formation. Eternal life begins in us when something of this life of the three divine persons happens also in our interiority. This happens through a knowing in faith of the life of the Trinity. This faith is your gift, Lord Jesus. You revealed that gift again to us in your priestly prayer at the last supper. Make our faith a living faith. Deepen our presence to God. Let us share more and more the mystery of your own presence to the Father in the Holy Spirit. Let us silently celebrate this presence in the depths of our being.

EPIPHANY OF MYSTERY

Epiphany of mystery
Silently embracing
Emergence of creation,
Transforming humanity
By gracious pervasion.
Mystery of gentle grace,
Illumine our ways,
Disclose the eternal exit
From the cage of time,
The empty, trying days,
A caravan of tired camels.
Eternal spark within
Pierce the dreary winter
Of forgetfulness of the Divine.
Clean the clouded window,
Weave threads of light
Through our nights.
Make us risk
The mysterious voyage
Of light and love.
Lighthouse, guide
Our little ships
Tossing on the churning
Waters of history.
Keep afloat the battered barks
Of fleeting lives.
Make us celebrate
Your presence in the depths
Of our being.

CHAPTER NINETEEN

A SONG OF THE NAME
AT THE END OF THE PERILOUS JOURNEY

I have glorified you on earth
and finished the work
that you gave me to do.   *(Jn.* 17:4)

Approaching the end of your life, you look gently back, Lord Jesus. Your life passes before your eyes. It has been good, very good. What else is life than a task to be fulfilled; the divine assignment of our short perilous journey in space and time. How short your journey was. Only thirty-three years. What counts is not the length of life but its beauty and intensity. Life is rich and deep when it is a song of gentle and firm fidelity to what the Father asks of us. Grant us the grace of insight, Jesus, into the mystery of our destiny. The great work of life cannot be reduced to any small task alone that we perform from day to day, such as doing the laundry, cleaning the dishes, dressing the children, writing a paper or building a house. To be sure, these works too are Father's will. You look at us with joy and love when we try to do them well as you did your daily chores in the little town of Nazareth. Yet somehow these small achievements have something to do with the life work the Father meant for us from eternity. We recall your own hidden life. Your play with other children, your learning of the Hebrew scriptures, your carpentry with St. Joseph and your helping of your mother with the household chores. They all had something to do with the life work the Father had given you to do. Yet none of these tasks in and by itself alone explains the fullness of the task that made your life uniquely yours.

A little further in this discourse you tell us what your life task was: "I have made your name known to the men you took from the world to give me." *(Jn.* 17:6)

Does our life task share in some way in that life task of yours? "Making Father's name known." What does that mean? What is Father's name? In the thought and feeling of the writers and readers of the Scriptures a name is not simply an external label attached to a person like an identification to a medicine bottle or a road sign to a road. For them a name expresses the unique mystery of the person and in the case of an eminent personality the name represents the greatness, glory and beauty that radiates forth from him. Making the name of the divine Father known means that our little life lets the beauty, truth and goodness of eternal life shine forth among people. You did this in ways we cannot equal. You did it most strikingly in the suffering and death awaiting you after this last supper. You did it eminently in your public speaking the last few years of your short and gentle life. But you also radiated his name in the hidden life of Nazareth. The infinite gentleness and generosity of your heavenly Father, the soft and mysterious splendor of his most holy name, the brightness of his glory was shining forth in

your smile and your word, in the flow of your
movements when you served at table, ran joyfully
with the other children in the market place, carried
the water jar for Mary or drove singing some shiny
nails in the polished wood of a table or chair or in the
plough of a simple farmer. The silent music of your
smile and movement sang the infinite beauty of the
Father. Our life too must be a song of the name.
Otherwise it would be lived in vain. For it would not
be a peaceful sharing in your eternal song to the
graciousness and glory of God. You ask us to radiate
Father's beauty into the succession of situations that
link our life together like a chain of pearls woven
uniquely for each of us by an eternal love.

For a few of us some of these situations may
appeal to a wider audience like it was for you in your
public life. Public recognition is a precarious gift, for
our pride will tempt us to let our own name shine
forth more than the name of the Father. Hence we are
grateful, Lord Jesus, when we are spared that temptation. Most of us are only called to the inconspicuous
life of Nazareth. Most of us are chosen to bring the
name of the Lord not in neon letters but in the
scribbles of a child; not in splendid oratory, but in
simple words of kindness and consolation; not in
heroic deeds of peace and justice that catch the
headlines, but in quiet fidelity to our family and daily
job. Most of us are not meant to shine in committee
meetings but to light a little candle of love in some
small corner of our neighborhood or working space.

The only thing that matters is that we in all small
things glorify Father's name on earth with you and
finish the work that he gave us to do.

If only we could say like you at the end of our
life: "I have glorified you on earth and finished the

work that you gave me to do." None of us ever can. All of us fail to live up to the heavenly burden. And yet we still can say it, because you will say it in us and for us. If we turn to you wholeheartedly in faith, hope and love at the moment of final transition.

You will spread a wonderful light of peace and mercy throughout the dying frame of our earthly existence. You forgive and complete what we did not do. In our dying and suffering body you sing to the eternal Father: In this poor sinner too I have glorified you on earth. My glorified humanity finishes at once before you Father the work that you gave this person to do. Please Father for my sake take this repentant soul in your eternal embrace of tender love. Remember Father that this soul too is one of those you gave to me from the world.

A SONG OF EVERLASTING PRAISE

Let me sing a song to your name
When I leave my frame
At the end of my perilous journey.
Let my breaking eyes look back
In sorrow at the dusty tracks
Of a life that failed so often
To fulfill the task you assigned.
Forgive my lack of fidelity
To the candle I was to be,
To keep alight your mystery
In a small corner of this earth.
Remind me of my destiny;
To let eternal life shine forth a little
In my own pedestrian way
Joyfully from day to day
Until the journey ends
And boundless light takes over silently.
Let the brightness of your glory
Sing in the music of movement and smile,
Of words of joy and animation;
A sharing in the song of praise
That is your risen life.
Show me in the light of faith
The procession of my life's events
As a chain of pearls
Woven tenderly by an eternal Love.
And when the journey ends
Sing for me to Father
Your dying song of everlasting praise
That makes my life complete for him
In spite of countless failures.

CHAPTER TWENTY

BEFORE THE WORLD EVER WAS

*Now, Father, it is time for you to glorify me
with that glory I had with you
before ever the world was.*   *(John* 17:5)

We adore the mystery of your intimacy with the Father, a mystery in which we share. A mystery that illumines our life in the shadows of the everyday and lifts us with you to where you are before the world ever was.

Your glory has been hidden from human eyes. But now at this last supper the moment is near when the veil of time will be lifted and the glory of eternity will explode in the battered frame of your bruised face and broken body. To heal us you hide your might and majesty. You suspend freely the glory that was yours before the world ever was.

At this last supper you know that this depletion of your infinite dignity will soon reach its awesome depth. Debasement is waiting you. But after your shameful death your humanity will rise to enduring glory. The glory already yours as the eternal word of God will shine forth unabated in your humanity.

We adore the boundless generosity of your divine love for our fallen and deformed race. What honor for this earth! This puny needlepoint whirling slowly in an immense universe, this pellet dwarfed by giant suns and vast stellar constellations. To think that an inhabitant of this tiny speck of stellar dust is invested with the full glory of the Creator of this overwhelming universe. Not an angel will be enthroned in divine resplendence but a human being with a human body, mind and heart, with human eyes, hand and feet, with gaping wounds will be divine. All the angels and archangels will lie prostrate in adoration of this divine human presence.

Why has this race been singled out by your Father for such lasting glory? Why not an angel, an archangel? Our voice falters, our mind is stunned, our hearts overcome by such love and honor for this strange and sinful population of lonely planet earth.

And yet your glorified humanity will not be alien to our humanity. Your humanity will transform ours. We shall be taken up in yours. Like a clear mountain lake reflects the beauty of the sun above it so will our redeemed humanity reflect your beauty. The Father will delight in your splendor that lights up in us. We will be your sparkling crown, Lord Jesus, for you have saved us by your blood.

"God, our Father, glorious in giving life and even more glorious in restoring it; when his last night on earth came, your Son shed tears of blood, but dawn brought incomparable gladness. Do not turn away from us, or we shall fall back into dust, but rather turn our mourning into joy by raising us up with Christ." (Holy Office, Ordinary Time, Week I, Thursday Evening Prayer)

Rising up in Christ, sharing his glory, that is our destiny in time and eternity.

That glory was yours, Jesus, before the world ever was. Was it mine also? Yes. In some sense I may say this in awed astonishment. Before I came to be in time I existed in eternity in the Father's vision of creation. In him radiated my face and form before I was born. That unique form loved by him so tenderly before all ages was to unfold in my life as his image in fleeting space and time. I have been preformed in the bosom of the Trinity. I was cradled in your gentle design before the world began, before you told the universe to explode in its terrifying splendor.

The preformation of the unique foundational form of my life was spoken eternally by the Father in his Divine Word in whom everything came to be.

In you, Eternal Word, I can find back in faith the articulation of the life form meant for me from eternity. In you too rests the mystery of the face that was mine before I was born and before the world ever began. That face that uniquely reveals the glory of God alone.

But we must admit in sorrow that the original form of glory did not reach full unfolding in any of us except the virgin in Nazareth and the son. The fall of humanity led to lasting deformation yet did not take away all possibility of some right formation of human life. Hence people of good will remain in painful search of lost paradise, of spoiled glory, of the secret stone of wisdom, the holy grail, the pearl of great price, the forgotten treasure of their inmost face and glorious form. We all feel the need of reformation of our scarred and misdirected lives. In some measure human reformation may succeed but never totally. We are wounded so deeply by our pride that only a

marvel of divine transformation can restore us to our
original splendor. St. Ignatius of Antioch exhorts us
so well: *"Look for him who is outside time, the eternal
one, the unseen, who became visible for us; he cannot
be touched and cannot suffer, yet he became subject
to suffering and endured so much for our sake."*

Inserting yourself, Divine Word, into our human
nature you begin to transform it from the inside out.
You save us from ugly deformations that cripple the
soul and soil heart and mind. You infuse us with your
glory and, wonder of wonders, you transform us into
real participants in the eternal formation event of the
Trinity. Assume us into your holy humanity. Make us
share in your own glory, the glory that was yours
before the world ever was. Then our face and form in
radiant transformation will show your face and form.
The Father will delight eternally in seeing your face
and form in ours.

THE FACE THAT WAS MINE

Before the world ever was
The song of birds, the green of grass,
The sun, the moon, the dance of stars,
The rivers, streams, the spruce and spars,
Before we were in woe and worry
There was the marvel of your glory.
We twinkled in its loving light,
Like little jewels in the bright
Prevision of what was to be
In time and in eternity.
O, the face that was mine
Before emerging in time.
The purity of form
That should be the norm
Of my unfolding life
Before anxious strife
Deformed my eternal beauty.
I refused the duty
Of forming life in your image Lord.
Yet embraced by your Word
I found the providential worth of everything
In life. The Word became the wing
That drew me gently home,
No longer lost, alone.
The Word became my transformation
In the marvel of your incarnation,
Revealing the form meant for me,
That flows from you, shall ever be.

CHAPTER TWENTY-ONE

THE NAME OF THE
RECKLESSLY TENDER ONE

I have made your name known
to the people you took from the world to give me.

(Jn. 17:6)

Holy Father,
keep those you have given me true to your name,
so that they may be one like us.

(Jn. 17:11)

How beautiful is the beginning of the second part
of your priestly prayer. Its melody of love reverberates in our inmost being. How infinite your care for
those you love. Each of us is entrusted to your
forming love by our Father in heaven. You pray for
the transformation of our lives in the splendor of his
image. We are given to you out of the world and the
deformative magic of its image of success. The world
threatens to seduce us with its prideful pulsations of
exaltation, perfectionism and cults of self-assertion.
Therefore, you pray explicitly for us who are given
to you.

This does not mean that you asked for your self alone, for your own glory, in the first part of your prayer. For that glory already embraces us too. First you asked the Father to give glory to your human life among us. What else is this glory than the consummation of your mission to our race? It is your eternal call to make Father's forming love wholly present to all people. You keep nothing for yourself alone. Nor do you receive anything for your own formation alone. The mutation of your humanity into everlasting glory means for you the possibility to let all people share in the transforming power of divine life. But you cannot say all these truths at once. For you share in our human nature. You share its limitations of thinking and speaking. Like us, you cannot at once express everything explicitly and simultaneously.

You can only now make more clear what the glory you ask for means to each of us. You want to make us aware what the glorious form of your humanity holds for your apostles and for us, your disciples. Then you let us see how we in turn are called to be the graced carriers, the joyful mediators, of your forming presence in the world.

With love and reverence you speak to us about the "name." "I have made your name known to the people . . . Holy Father keep them true to your name."

Somebody may ask, "What is in a name?" It is manifest that you want to share with us an enchanting mystery in speaking so lovingly about the name. Some tribal people are expert in the art of naming. Being together for a long time in the intimacy of the tribal community, they are often able to express in one striking name the lasting core form of each other's life.

Similarly, people in love may find endearing names for one another. They express in that name some core quality that only love discloses in the beloved. It is a name only they may know. They may want to keep it between them because it reveals something of the secret of their life. Even if the revealing name would be spoken publicly, others could not fully penetrate its deeper meaning. For they would not have shared the history of love between people who named each other in this unveiling fashion.

Something similar, Lord, has happened in the enchanting love story between your Father and the people he formed in love, the God of Abraham, Isaac and Jacob. In infinite generosity your Father unveiled for them his name. It was a mysterious name: Jahwe: I am the "I am." What was surprising was not only the name itself but the fact that God allowed them to call him by his name.

At that period of history people felt that they had power over those whose intimate name they could master, for they would know the secret of their strength. They assumed that the all-mighty divinity would remain unspeakable and could never be named. How startled they were that your Father allowed them to call him by a name which he himself revealed to them. For them it was an awesome demonstration of your Father's trust. And yet we learn from your prayer that this early gift of a divine name was only a vague beginning of your Father's self-unveiling.

Nobody has ever brought God so near to us as you, Lord Jesus. His forming presence was never made more intimately known to us than in you, his son, who took on our wounded flesh. *I have made your name known to the people.* You opened for people a whole new path to the heart of Divinity. The revelation you gave us about God's being is not so much in what you say but in what you are. Your very being among us gives a new depth to the human words you use. The word Father had been applied to God long before your appearance on earth. But nowhere could this familiar symbol gain the mysterious depth and overwhelming beauty you granted it by your living of the name.

Your incarnation compelled you to express yourself only in words familiar to us. So you use the familiar word Father for God. But what you unveil by means of common parlance is infinitely original. It could only be communicated by you, lovely splendor of the eternal light. You transform the power of language like you transform people. You revealed to us the depth of meaning of the symbol "Father." You made it a whole new word for us. You did so by revealing that you are the son who is in his very being like the Father. You let us see in your own humanity that God has loved the world as no one could have imagined or thought out cleverly. Your life alone makes the forming Fatherhood of God transparent to humanity.

Our human experience of fatherhood is distorted. Many fathers fail their calling. Many lack fidelity to the formative presence they are called to be for those entrusted to their care. Even the best among them are limited in generosity, patience and compassion. No human father can express fully the loving presence of your Father to our daily misery. Only you could be the living expression of that presence. You could truly say: "Who sees me sees the Father."

To be formed in you is to be lifted beyond the formation history of our father-experience. Your presence purifies it from its pain and limitation. When we allow you to whisper within us, Abba Father, a whole new world opens up — a world we call heaven. *Our Father,* who art in *heaven.* How we love and adore with you the name that points to the inexpressable mystery of divine fatherhood: *hallowed be thy name.* Your Father's love is so all-encompassing, sweet and gentle that it contains the tenderness symbolized too by motherhood. God is eminently father *and* mother for us as is manifested movingly in the life of you, Lord Jesus, who are his incarnated love.

Thank you most tender Lord for making the Father appear to us by manifesting yourself as the Son. For nobody can know the Father without you. Have mercy on us when we imagine we know him while neglecting to abide with you. What do we know of him aside from you? We may acknowledge him reverently as Creator, as Judge, as the Almighty. But this ancient form in which God appears is limited and onesided. It does not temper our hidden fear, our secret trembling because it implies that he may only be the anxiety-evoking, the punishing, the terrifying, the incomprehensible one. How many became nonbelievers to escape this dread that paralyzed their life? It is awful to face the Almighty without the prism of your presence, Jesus.

We may claim to meet God more easily in nature than in Church and Scripture. Yet nature is only a flawed manifestation of the Infinite. Nature is not only enchanting, noble and sublime. Nature is also merciless, cruel, a source of catastrophes and savage pain.

Without you, Lord Jesus, there is a dizzying distance between the Father and us. Nothing can bridge the abyss that separates us: he is all powerful, we powerless; he is saintliness, we are sin; he is purity, we corruption; he is Wisdom Infinite, we small-mindedness; he is just and generous; we are dishonest, mean and greedy. There is no bridge, no exit from our mean condition, no entrance into the mystery of Father's generosity without your humanity. You alone could disclose to us the deepest meaning of the name of the recklessly tender One, the lovely name of Father.

A MELODY OF TENDER LOVE

A melody of tender love
Sings in my inmost being,
The sweet and snowy dove
Of love dwells in my deepest feeling.
The splendor of the living Lord
Lights up the Father's name.
When lived by the Eternal Word
This word is not the same
As it was known before
In common word and speech.
It was only symbol, metaphor
Of Love beyond my reach.
Then you descended in my life,
O mediator of the name.
You kindled in my weary heart
The everlasting flame
Dancing between you and him,
Lifting me beyond my power,
Pushing me beyond the rim
Of any mental tower
Of wisdom, strength and might
Built by human thought,
Clever, straight and right
And yet not wrought
By you alone, my God.
Thank you for this sweet unveiling
Of what transcends the human tongue.
Let us not be failing
The Father for whom we long,
For whom we pine so desperately,
The Father we lose unknowingly
When we transfer our search for you
To failing fathers here on earth.

CHAPTER TWENTY-TWO

GIFTS OF UNSPEAKABLE GRACE

"They were yours and you gave them to me."

(Jn. 17:6)

Lord, you allow us again to glimpse the intimacy and mystery of the life of the Trinity: "They were yours . . . " What a joy to experience in your words that we are truly his. We were pre-formed in the formative love of the Father from all eternity: "They *were* yours . . . " With the word *were* you don't mean to say that we are no longer the treasured creatures of the Father, formed tenderly in his image and likeness. We were, we are, we will always be his children. You want to express in these words that from now on we are given to your holy humanity by the Father to be yours in a new way.

We were already yours before your incarnation, suffering and death. As the Divine Word of the Father, you — as the Expression of his fulness — hold within yourself from eternity all that exists and pre-exists in his caring and creative love. We too are held in that pre-forming and forming love of the Father. Therefore, we are also held in you, his Eternal

Word, before all ages, before the explosive formation in time of this awesome universe that dwarfs our passing existence in space and time. And yet you made us infinitely more than this universe. For your Father called us from eternity into Eternity. We lost this privilege of an everlasting joyful presence before his face, but in his faithful love he sent you to transform our radically deformed lives. He gave us to you to present us to him unblemished because of your transfiguring presence in us.

We have been handed over to you, Lord Jesus. You are the incarnated and incarnating formation mystery that surrounds and permeates suffering humanity. We have been given to you and you in turn give us back to the Father in a whole new way. That way is *you,* for as you have said so clearly: I am the way.

. . . and they have kept your word.
Now at last they know
that all you have given me comes indeed from you;
for I have given them
the teachings you gave to me,
and they have truly accepted this, that I came from you,
and have believed that it was you who sent me.

(Jn. 17:6-8)

The Father gave us to you, incarnated divine mystery of human transformation. But he left to us the freedom of refusing to be Father's gift to you. We reject ourselves as his gift if we resist your loving power of transformation. Divine created and uncreated powers of formation emanate from the Trinity. Their mystical tide sweeps invisibly through space and time, through universe, world, humanity and history. They surround, inundate and permeate all that is and becomes. They give rise to countless current forms of life and matter.

The divine forming powers find their highest form and expression in the Father's enfleshed Eternal Word. The mysterious intensity of this divine transforming power is condensed in your words that are the words of the Father. You ask us only to allow that word into our hearts, to cherish and keep it, to dwell on it without ceasing.

If we keep it inwardly, it will explode like the power of a split atom. Dwelling in the word we shall be transformed inwardly. We shall be in tune again with the divine created and uncreated forming powers always at work in history. True, we lost touch with them, but to keep your word is to come in touch again.

Keeping your word as Mary did in her heart leads to an enlightened awareness of your forming presence, Lord Jesus. Through your grace we taste in your word, kept inwardly and outwardly, that you are the Eternal Word, co-equal with the Father. At last we know in faith-experience that the Father pours out from eternity in you the fullness of his divinity, that the Father and you are one. In the light and the darkness of faith, we truly accept and adore your divinity and its incarnational, forming mystery in our lives. Then you say:

> I pray for them;
> I am not praying for the world
> but for those you have given me,
> because they belong to you:
> all I have is yours
> and all you have is mine,
> and in them I am glorified.
> I am not in the world any longer,
> but they are in the world,
> and I am coming to you.

I kept those you had given me true to your name.
I have watched over them and not one is lost
except the one who chose to be lost,
and this was to fulfill the scriptures.

(Jn. 17:1-13)

Now, Lord Jesus, you are offering a prayer for us alone. You say expressly: "I am not praying for the world but for those you have given me." You make us feel in gratefulness that we have been chosen out of the world. We are truly God's gift to you. You return us to the Father and make us share in that eternal interformative relationship, which is the essence of the divine unity. You tell us in your prayer that you are glorified in us.

How moving it is to see your loyalty to your friends around the table of this Last Supper. It is even more touching when we realize that you knew that they would break away from you and desert you as we so often do. And yet what is even more touching is your unmistakable pride in them and in us: " . . . and in them I am glorified."

In spite of our infidelities and countless deformations, you still have pride in us. In spite of our shame and guilt, you not only have pride in us, but you express your gratitude to God for us. For all through your prayer you keep speaking of your disciples and their followers as a gift of the Father to you: " . . . those you have given me." That expression comes back again and again throughout your prayer. Over and over you praise God's generosity to you. It is as if you cannot get away from that praise. We speak of you as the Father's unspeakable gift to us, but you, incredibly enough, seem to delight in us as an amazing gift from the Father to you.

It sounds overwhelming. That the Eternal Word should bother about the transformation of our life is wonder enough. Why should you squander the fullness of your own human life to foster our possibility for transformation? You allow your life to be cut short thereby drastically limiting the formation possibility open to your own gifted humanity? Why should you devote your life to our transformation? And yet unaccountably, in spite of our infidelity, you seem to esteem us as a priceless gift of the Father. You do everything for us and the only advantage you reap is that we are transformed.

Truly, no formative friend or director can ever be as loyal as you are, Lord Jesus. How ashamed we feel of our carelessness about the gracious gift of your formative presence. The Father has put you in the midst of the drama of our daily life formation. How unaware humanity is of how you have filled and enriched its formation history. Lovingly and trustfully, you commit us to the Father's watchfulness and care.

> But now I am coming to you
> and while still in the world I say these things
> to share my joy with them to the full.
> I passed your word on to them,
> and the world hated them,
> because they belong to the world
> no more than I belong to the world.
> I am not asking you to remove them from the world,
> but to protect them from the evil one.
> They do not belong to the world
> any more than I belong to the world.

(Jn. 17:13-16)

You tell the Father that you say all of these things to share your joy with us to the full. The ground of our formation in and with you is the peace and joy we experience in the core of our being in spite of the hate we may feel from the world which resists your forming ways. We should never expect that fidelity to your forming ways will gain us admiration in the world of mere human ambition and earthly aspiration. However, you do not want the Father to remove us from the world. We have to radiate your presence in the midst of the world as a reminder of the grace that is promised to all. You ask the Father only to protect us in the world from the evil one, who constantly tries to seduce us away from you. Being in the midst of the world yet not being in the world, we exemplify how the good things of this earth and the achievements of human history can be taken up in the glorious form of life you have meant for humanity from eternity.

ODE TO THE TRINITY

Mystery of the Trinity
Whose forming mutuality
Fills us with adoration.
O mutual generation
Of intimacy
We are called to share.
How can we bear
The awe, the gratefulness
That floods our being
Preformed by your tenderness,
Whispered into your Word Divine
Who became the Lord benign
In space and time
In which we travel awkwardly,
Dwarfed by the splendid terror
Of a universe that outshines
The shaken heart, the feeble mind.
Yet only we are called
From eternity into Eternity,
Only our dust is given
To the Word's humanity
As a lasting home,
Transfiguring us
Into unblemished beauty
Before your delighted eye.
Mighty currents of formation
Emanate from You, O Trinity;
A mystical tide
Sweeps invisibly
Through space and time,
Humanity and history,
Inundating all becoming,
Giving rise to countless forms
Of life and matter,
Synchronized in the Father's
Enfleshed Eternal Word
In whom we dwell,
Who dwells in us
Lifting us lovingly
Into your mystery,
O Trinity.

CHAPTER TWENTY-THREE

THE CONSECRATION OF
THE HOUSE OF HISTORY

Consecrate them in the truth;
your word is truth.
As you send me into the world,
I have sent them into the world,
and for their sake I consecrate myself
so that they too may be consecrated in truth.

(Jn. 17:17-19)

Lord, you pray for the consecration of our lives. What is this consecration? It is transformation of life by the divine love of the Father. He wants us to be transformed in your image as bread and wine are transformed by consecration into your holy body and blood. You want us to flow with this invitation, to yield to the wonder of consecration in our lives. You ask us to dedicate and abandon our human formation to the divine mystery of formation. The mystery answers our plea with consecration: the transformation of our life into the image and likeness of the Most High and the Most Deep. As Psalm 24 sings:

Gates, raise your arches,
rise, you ancient doors,
let the king of glory in!

The gates of our human faith, hope and love are lifted beyond their boundaries; the ancient doors to our interiority grow higher by your consecration. Widened by grace, they enable you, the king of glory, to enter the formation histories of our lives, fleeting moments in space and time. You not only enter our lives but all that surrounds and nourishes them, your dwelling place. "How dear to me, your dwelling place, Lord God of hosts." *(Ps.* 84:2)

Yes my Lord, I believe that the formation history of universe, world and humanity is your dwelling place. How dear has this house of history become to me since you revealed it to be the house of the Lord God of hosts. Hosts not only of angels but also the hosts of atoms and subatomic particles in which you poured your forming power at the beginning. You are the Lord of the hosts of particles that in an uninterrupted mating dance give form to universe and world and to my life embedded in this concert of formation that spans the aeons of time.

"How holy is the sanctuary of the Most High. God fills it with his presence and eternal strength." *(Ps.* 84) Today we may call it the sanctuary of the Most High and Most Deep, of the Transcendent and the Immanent. You disclosed to us indirectly through the gifted minds of generations of thinkers and scientists that at the heart of universe, world and humanity is the mysterious presence of a formative power. It is the power of the mystery of formation, a divine energy emanating from you, eternal Trinity, into the bosom of matter, space and time. You fill this always ongoing formation with your presence and eternal strength. Hence the psalmist also cries out: "My heart and my flesh sing for joy to the living God". *(Ps.* 84) Our heart, body, organism — an awe-inspiring outcome of the formation history of millenia — exult in your living presence in this ongoing miracle of formation.

In the fullness of time you lift our gates, you make the ancient doors grow higher, you softly enter, king of glory, if we don't resist your descent in our lives like snow flakes in winter or cherry blossoms in spring.

Through us you want to enter the house of history in a way that is new, consecrating and healing. Consecrated by your presence, you want us to consecrate the world. You ask us to dedicate to the Father all the formation processes and events that make up nature, humanity and history. You cry out: "If any man is thirsty, let him come to me! Let the man come and drink who believes in me!" *(Jn.* 7:37-38)

Streams of living faith, hope and love flow out from our consecrated hearts. They nourish the rivers of justice, peace and compassion that facilitate the abandonment of all hearts to the unique formation the Spirit means for them.

You want us to dedicate all that exists to the divine formation mystery. Such dedication is symbolized in people and things traditionally consecrated to the Most High and the Most Deep, altars, temples, priests and sacrifices.

How generous of the Father to invite us to share in his loving act of transforming consecration, to call us to dedicate people, things, events to his holy presence in creation.

In this prayer, Lord Jesus, you dedicate first of all your own life to the Father. You acknowledge your own priestly power of transforming consecration. You announce hereby that your suffering and dying will be a dedicating sacrifice. Your holy passion is a priestly consecration that embraces the consecration to which we are all invited.

You pray: "So that they too may be consecrated in truth." What is this mysterious truth in which we are called to be consecrated? You explain it in the words: "Consecrate them in the truth; your word is truth." God's word is truth. It is the self-communication of the Eternal. You disclose to us that we will be transformed by sharing in that divine self-revelation. You include in that truth the whole wonder of the Father's forming and transforming word, the whole mystery of formation.

The divine formation power flows from the inner and inter-formation of the Trinity into the outer-formation of universe, world, history and humanity. It reaches its full expression in time in you, incarnate Word of the Father. We adore you as the Truth, as containing and expressing the full reality of the Divinity.

Formation as consecration in and by the divine truth embraces all of our life. In this transformation you make us a source of consecration for others. You send us into the world as you have been sent by the Father. "As you sent me into the world, I have sent them into the world." Help us Jesus to be faithful to this mission. Make us gently pursue excellence in the profession and position you assigned to us in the world. Make us just, peaceful and compassionate wherever you allow us to be inserted into the history of humanity.

THE HOUSE OF HISTORY

Make me yield, my Lord
To the Word
Of consecration,
Of transformation
Of my ways
Melted by the rays
Of your compassion.
May the gates of my life
Lift high their heads,
May the ancient doors
Of mind and heart
Grow higher still,
Open to your will
To enter
The still center
Of this moment,
This shy event
I am in space and time.
Bring victory
To the house of history
In which you dwell.
You are the well
Of the mating dance
Of atomic dust,
This dynamic thrust
Forming the universe
In aeons of time
That follow each other
Like camels
In the deserts
Of empty spaces,
Leaving behind
The traces
Of surging, dying
Planets, stars.

In the end
You descend
Like snow
In winter,
Like blossoms
In spring
Fall softly
From their branches.
You are the spring
Within of living waters
Rising to the brim
Of our hearts
To flow into humanity
Thirsty for consecration
And compassion.

CHAPTER TWENTY-FOUR

FEEBLE ECHOES OF
THE ETERNAL GENERATION

I pray not only for these,
but for those also
who through their words will believe in me.
May they all be one.
Father, may they be one in us,
as you are in me and I am in you,
so that the world may believe it was you who sent me.
I have given them the glory you gave to me
that they may be one as we are one.
With me in them and you in me,
may they be so completely one
that the world will realize that it was you who sent me
and that I have loved them as much as you loved me.

(Jn. 17:20-23)

Your prayer holds an invitation. You wish us to dwell in the luminosity of the mystery of mysteries. You pray that we may enter into the eternal formation Event: the most Holy Trinity. You ask us to image among us this formation Event. You want us to recreate it in our loving communion with one another. Only in you, Lord can we restore in the Christian community the image of eternal Love.

Please, let it be restored and radiate forth in humanity, let us share in the loving communion between you, the Father and the Holy Spirit. The Trinitarian Event can only become ours through a priceless gift of transformation you alone can grant.

We adore the mysterious community of one divine nature. We marvel at the dynamism of Love that forms the inner life of the divinity. This inner formation is an eternal process of interformation of Three Persons within this absolute community. In thanksgiving we commemorate the creative outflow of this divine formation in outer formation in time and space. For the same eternal Love gave form to universe, world and history which you meant to be the womb of the interformative community of humanity. For humanity is called to image and share your Trinitarian Formation Event in time and eternity.

You wanted to give us some awareness of the source of the mystery of formation we are embraced by at every moment of our lives. For in this Trinitarian mystery is hidden the source of the forming powers of life and universe. If you Father would not have formed from eternity the Son, there would have been no formation of the world. This marvel of the cosmos, this astonishing wealth of forming forces and processes is only a feeble echo of the formation of the Son out of you, loving Father of the universe. Your stream of formation flows through your eternal Word into the formation of universe, world, humanity and history.

Your Spirit moved the writers of the holy book to sing of this mystery:

> Through him all things came to be,
> not one thing had its being but through him.

(Jn. I:3)

He is the image of the unseen God
and the first-born of all creation,
for in him were created
all things in heaven and on earth: . . .
all things were created through him and for him.

(Col. I-15:16)

The creative formation of universe and humanity flowed from your Eternal Formation Event. Your infinitely deeper creation within this creation is the Christian community. You raised it up in the midst of the history of human formation as a center of joyous transformation. Within it you assembled compassionately all those redeemed by our Lord. This transformative union of Christians too is a mystery like that of your Trinitarian life. Our community in him has been preformed in your Eternal Formation Event: *Before the world was formed, he chose us, chose us in Christ, to be holy and spotless, and to live through love in his presence. (Eph. I:4)*

Some beautiful traces of the transformative power of the Christian community may be seen by human eyes. Their divine source, however, remains veiled from mere human understanding. This hiddenness of the sacred source reminds us of the wonder of your own presence among the people of Israel. Many marvelled at the fruits of your encounter. Yet only your gift of faith could disclose to them that these fruits sprang from your eternal immersion in the Trinitarian Formation Event. The same is true of us, the community of your faithful. Together we are called to be co-formed with you in the same Eternal Formation Event. Our faith in this silent, inward transformation starts out from what we see and hear. Only your gift of faith, however, enables us to see the formation of your own life and that of ours in a whole new light. Christian life formation is disclosed to us as a striking expression in space and time of the mystery of divine formation. For you are in us *the image of the unseen God. (Col.* I:15)

When we meditate on this prayer which you spoke at the end of your life, we begin to realize how you bring together all past and future treasures that flow from your dwelling among us in the flesh. You pray first for your disciples who accept and cherish your word. Then your prayer embraces each of us. *You pray for all those who through their words will believe in me.* You ask for us *may they all be one.* You grant us an understanding of this Christian unity: *Father, may they be one in us, as you are in me and I am in you.*

You disclose the divine source of our unity: The Trinitarian Formation Event. *As you Father are in me and I am in you.* Our union with one another is to be achieved in that image; it is the divine archetype of graced interformation.

How can we be in one another like you and the Father are in one another? It is, of course, not a material, spatial being in one another, like a tree is in the ground, a flower in a vase, a star in the sky. You speak here about a far more intimate being in one another, a spiritual in-being, a meeting of what is deepest in all of us, ultimately of you in us. To reach that depth of being in one another, we must go beyond the way we see one another in daily life or like one another in a jovial, convivial fashion. No matter how good this is, it is still far from the unity-in-depth you envision here.

These everyday ways of knowing and liking are an expression of our vital and functional togetherness in daily life. You appeal here to our highest power of loving and knowing that transcends mere functional and vital powers of knowing and liking. You elevate those transcendent powers of ours by the pneumatic gifts of your Holy Spirit. Typical of this unique highest power of understanding and loving is that they permeate one another. Blended like the ray of a lazer beam, they radiate out in unity from the transformed center of our being. When you direct gently this unique blend of loving understanding or understanding love at other human beings, it appeals to the deepest possibilities you implanted in them. If they are open they experience the warmth of an enlightened knowing of the human heart.

Only this graced blend of spiritual love and understanding allows us to empathize with the divine uniqueness in one another, to be in the center of one another as you are in the Father and the Father is in you. Thank you, Lord, for not only painting the ideal but for granting us the power of its realization. For you enable us to share in the formative love of the three Divine Persons for one another and for humanity. You invite and enable us to see each other with the look with which your Father gazes at you, and you, eternal Word, contemplate your Father. You ask us to love one another as the Father loves you, the Son, and you the Father. Only when you grant us a participation in this divine blend of love and understanding can we mature beyond the oppositions and aggravations between us.

You are in me and I am in you. You do not mean to encapsulate us in a closed circle of committed Christians, a gnostic enclave of the elect. You want us to care passionately for justice, peace and mercy, also for those outside our community. Twice in this passage you pray for our openness to the world: *so that the world may believe that you have sent me. May they be so completely one that the world will realize that it was you who sent me.*

Such selfless care of the Christian community — combined with the witness of its own internal loving unity — may move the hearts of people more than anything else. The world suffers under the dissension and distrust, the mutual battles of a divided and divisible humanity. Many people of good will strive wholeheartedly for peace, mutual understanding, human encounter, world unity, loving harmony. Yet the human vulnerability for the divisiveness that followed the Fall can be relieved but never totally overcome by excellent intentions, marvellous slogans, peace marches and conferences, disarmaments, sensitivity training courses and group dynamics alone. They all can be helpful. They should be realized insofar as possible. But they will never be sufficient by themselves alone to surpass totally our basic disunity.

Your grace of unity is needed. Help us to allow this grace to manifest itself in our loving Christian community. Enable us to *bear with one another charitably, in complete selflessness, gentleness and patience . . . to preserve the unity of the spirit by the peace that binds together. (Eph.* IV:2-4) Let us *all grow into one holy temple in the Lord; . . . being built into a house where God lives, in the Spirit. (Eph. II:22)* Then we shall attract others into the light of our transforming community like restless flying creatures are attracted from the darkness of the falling night into the light circle of an evening lamp. They will pray together: stay with us, Lord for it is nearly evening and the day is almost over *(Luke* 24:29-30). In our community of interformation, they will recognize you with us in the breaking of the bread.

A SHRINE IN TIME

Mysterious Trinity,
Make us dwell
In the clarity
Of the well
Of what is to be.
Do not wait
To recreate
The image
Of divine formation
In us, who believe in you.
Make us a shrine in time
In which you shine
Splendidly.
You are the womb
Of history, the image
Of what humanity
Might be.
What else are we
Than feeble echoes
Of the generation
Of the eternal Son,
The Archetype, the Spring,
Of all formation,
The hesitant inhabitants
Of your redeeming Light,
Elected to be a center of transformation
At the heart of history,
Glowing traces
Of the embraces
Of the Divine Event,
Rays of the lazer beam
Of love divine
In sordid time.

Presence is paralyzed
By profanity.
Finally,
The closed enclave
Of the elect
Empties out
In the teeming streets
Of the divided city
To share with passers-by
Your harmony
O Trinity.

CHAPTER TWENTY-FIVE

THE PANORAMIC VISION

Father,
I want those you have given me
to be with me where I am,
so that they may always see the glory
you have given me
because you loved me
before the foundation of the world.
Father, Righteous One,
the world has not known you,
but I have known you,
and these have known
that you have sent me.
I have made your name known to them
and will continue to make it known,
so that the love with which you loved me
        may be in them,
and so that I may be in them.

(Jn. 17:24-26)

Your last discourse, Lord, is like the final song of
your life's formation. It is the tale of what your life
has been, what is is to be, how it shall shine forth in
our history. Your prayer has been a rhythmic repeti-
tion of the truths of formation. Each new expression

deepens their meaning. They are to guide the journey of humanity.

You depart but promise to join again our history in your Holy Spirit. He will direct us in our formative adventure, enabling us to add a pneumatic dimension to our power of appraisal of people, events and things. It is crucial to appraise them in his sublime light for they make up the life situations that form us and those to which we give form.

Your prayer is not a syllogism of the mind but a poem of the heart. Each formative meaning you disclose is a dynamic spiral of truth. One directive meaning spirals powerfully into another.

At the center of your prayerful attention are the "Father and you" like the sun shines, life-giving and powerful, in the midst of its planets. In and around the mystery of Father and you the disciples are invited as a first circle of participants in that mystery. Then you ask Father to lift gently within that circle the community of those who follow you. Lastly, we pray for the world not yet believing in you, still called to share with us the miracle of transformation.

The finale of your prayer resumes these themes. The mystery of divine formation was the message of your farewell discourse as a whole. You bring it all together here in one panoramic vision. Prayerfully you again let this mystery unfold itself, spiral forth out of its inmost core.

The heart of this spiral of meanings is in your words: *You loved me before the foundation of the world . . . I have known you.*

You disclose again the mystery of interformation between the Father and you. To bring it nearer to us you highlight its dynamics with words familiar to us in daily life: to love and to know. The presence of the Father to you is here called "loving." Your responsive presence to the Father's love is described by you as "knowing," "acknowledging." You have told us elsewhere that to know and to love include one another in the relationship between the Father and you. *(Jn.* 14, 31; *Mt.* 11, 27)

The words loving and knowing can be used interchangeably to describe the dynamics of this divine interformation. Both the Father and you are equally loving and knowing each other in eternity. Yet there you emphasize the loving aspect of Father's presence to you, and the knowing and acknowledging aspect of your presence to him. You are praying here to the Father not as his eternal but as his incarnate son.

"Acknowledging Father's love" points to your part in the interformation in time between your eternal Father and you-as-human emerging in, among and with us in creation. As human you acknowledge adoringly the love of the Father giving form to your humanity. He has formed you with a love that embraced your humanity before the world was founded and formed. As human you show us in your prayer how we too should respond to the creative and forming love of the Father.

He loved us first. Deeply we were loved by him before we could love and know him. Our love for him can only be a response to a love that is already there, encompassing all we are and aspire to be. The foundation of our presence with you to the Father is the acknowledgment of this wonder of love that makes us be, that was with us before the world was.

On basis of this graced acknowledgment we become able to respond in love to Love. We do so by giving some concrete form to the loving presence of God in this world. Only in that sense can we speak of our *interforming* presence to God. We cannot form God as God. But we are generously called by your Father to co-form the concrete manifestations of his divine, dynamic presence in world, humanity and history. We can only do so in and with you, Lord Jesus. *And these have known that you have sent me. I have made your name known to them.*

The disciples sharing your table, listening to your words in silent wonder deep down know that you are sent by the Father. In their heart of hearts they know that you are more than a sublime teacher of subtle truth, more than an unsurpassed example of consonant life formation, more than a great prophet in Israel. You appear in all these ways. You are truly all of them and yet infinitely transcend them. Your Father granted your disciples the grace to grow beyond their perception of these apparent and current forms of your life. Grace enabled them to penetrate to the core of your existence, your unique foundational form of life, the very mystery of your being.

You know that in their heart they sense and acknowledge the inmost source and secret of your life's formation. This unique secret of your being is the interformative union of you and your Father. This eternal union between the Father and you, the Word, has now become also an interformative relationship in time between the Father and your humanity.

For the Father has sent you. His sending gives form to each moment and mode of your daily life. We are called to both your divine formation mystery in time and in eternity. The secret of your divine life formation becomes the secret of our own transformation. What is formative for you becomes transformative for us. Our own human formation potential must be transformed and elevated by Father's grace to share in your power of divine formation. Your deepest longing for us, Lord Jesus, is to share with us the life of divine interformation so that it might be ours too in fullness and in truth.

Your life is the joy of knowing intimately that you receive all forms of life, all their dimensions and articulations from the Father alone, that it is the work of his hands, that he is the rock on which your life unfolds in its fragile beauty. It is your joy to acknowledge in thought and feeling, image, word and deed this gift of divine formation which is the same as an ongoing divine sending. Your life is the joy of letting this acknowledgment blossom out in thanksgiving, love and adoration like fields of flowers open up under the rays of the sun in early spring. Your song of acknowledgment is a grateful appraisal of the gift of formation. This appreciation is the beginning of the concrete implementation of the gift in your daily life with others.

The moment you touch us with this life of joyful appreciation we begin to know with you something of the name, the being, the interforming life of the Trinity. It is a modest beginning that you will expand and deepen when we become more intimate with you during our life in the Christian community. Therefore you not only say: *I have made your name known to them.* You add to it: *and will continue to make it known, so that the love with which you loved me may be in them, and so that I may be in them.*

Your promise of continuation of your transforming message announces the new eon, the time of the Christian community, the millenia of graced transformation of humanity. You invite us to enter into that community of transformation through faith and baptism. You have made clear to us that this entrance entails a leaving behind of mere worldly formation. You know that the fund of secular formation directives the world offers us can never lead us to the glorious final form of life to which the Trinity calls us gently and constantly.

You have warned us also that worldly formation is contaminated by the pride form of life. Pride resists the gift of divine formation by your Holy Spirit. Your divine formation infinitely transcends worldly formation yet includes and elevates the best human formation has to offer. In this ending of your farewell message you mention once more this world: *Father, Righteous One, the world has not known you.* The insufficiency of the world is due to its refusal to acknowledge that you are sent by the Father, the One right source of the formation of world and history. Your mission by this Righteous One is the crucial event in the formation history of humanity. Outside its acknowledgment no right course of life and world formation will be revealed to us.

Make us withstand the pulsations of the world of self-sufficiency. Enable us to receive the continuation of your message in our lives. Deepen our intimate knowledge and graced experience of the interformation mystery between you and the Father.

You have disclosed to us that the interforming power of love between you and the Father gives rise to a third Person, the Holy Spirit. He is the interforming Love in Person. Therefore, where you and the Father are present in interformation there is also necessarily present the Spirit. The Holy Spirit is the gift of your interformative Love to our life and to our Christian community. You say, therefore, that *the* love with which you loved me may be in them. Your statement reminds us of St. Paul's: *the love of God has been poured into our hearts by the Holy Spirit which has been given us. (Rm. 5:5)*

Father, I want those you have given me to be where I am so that they may always see the glory you have given me.

Father, you created universe and world as a dynamic movement of rising and dying forms, interacting in a mysterious consonance no human mind can fathom in its totality in time and space. On this planet you made human existence form itself as an increasingly free and conscious movement of formation within, with and yet above the formation story of your universe. In giving form with you in the unfolding world, we ourselves are formed in a marvelous interplay with the powers of formation in and around us. You invite us to grow from current life form to current life form. Under your loving direction we are called to spiral forth from freedom to freedom until we are granted the full disclosure of the foundational life form you meant for us before the foundation of the world.

Since the Fall, we are unable by ourselves alone to realize that final joyous and glorious form of life. Daily we are pained, by a transcendent vision of glory we are unable to attain. Thank you for sending us your Son to transform our feeble formation attempts into a path towards the glorious form of life to which we innately aspire.

Thank you, Lord Jesus, for asking the Father that we who are given to you may be where you are. You are in the eternal embrace of the Father, sharing the light and love of divinity. They burst out in nameless glory, a flaming manifestation of the fullness of divine joy and beauty. And you ask the Father for us that we may always see the raiments of glory with which the Father has clothed your wounded humanity. We can only see or experience your glory intimately by sharing it.

You are thus really asking the Father to make us share your glory forever. Your glory will not absorb our uniqueness. We will never totally be you. An infinite distance will always reign between us and divinity even in the midst of this sharing in your elevation. For each of us to share uniquely the glory of your transformed and risen humanity is to attain the final and glorious unique life form to which each of us aspires.

To receive this final gift in the Eschaton we must trustingly see and share the hiddenness of your glory here on earth. Earthly eyes may only see suffering and humiliation, feebleness and failure where the eyes of faith see our transformation into glory by sharing in Jesus' passion. Help us to abandon ourselves to you in the night of detachment from worldly glory. Unveil to us your loving divinity within your suffering humanity. Grant us glimpses of your light during our journey on earth, consoling previews of the glories to be revealed in our eternal intimacy with your risen humanity. Is that not the vision your Spirit moved John to write about in this gospel. Already in the prologue he announces this glory: *We saw his glory, the glory that is his as only Son of the Father, full of grace and truth. (Jn.* 1:14)

THE PANORAMIC VISION

Your Spirit moves in history
The journey of humanity,
Its hesitant adventure
Into lands unknown
Hidden in the undergrowth
Of stale convention.
Lifted gently in the circle
Of yours and Father's mystery
Let us enjoy
The panoramic vision
Of the miracle of formation
Unfolding from the core
Of dynamic Trinity,
Flowing out into creation,
Sparkling forth in myriad forms
That rise and fall
In time and space
Until the human race
Emerges as participant
In your formation of the world.
You are the rock
On which our life unfolds
In fragile beauty.
We open up
Like flowers do in early spring,
Pollinated by the dusty wing
Of the gentle bee
That is the Spirit,
Fertilizing human minds
With divine appreciation,
From which deeds are born
That transform
Humanity and its suffering.
They dull the sting of pride.
With the wounded humanity of Jesus
We are clothed
In the raiments of his glory.